Times and Tendencies

TIMES AND TENDENCIES

BY
AGNES REPPLIER

Essay Index Reprint Series

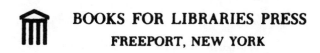

BOOKS FOR LIBRARIES PRESS
FREEPORT, NEW YORK

INTERNATIONAL STANDARD BOOK NUMBER:
0-8369-2028-7

LIBRARY OF CONGRESS CATALOG CARD NUMBER:
71-128297

PRINTED IN THE UNITED STATES OF AMERICA

Note

(TO THE ORIGINAL EDITION)

SEVEN of the twelve essays in this volume, 'Cure-Alls,' 'What is Moral Support,' 'On a Certain Condescension in Americans,' 'Actor and Audience,' 'The Public Looks at Pills,' 'The Unconscious Humour of the Movies,' and 'A Vocabulary,' are reprinted through the courtesy of the *Atlantic Monthly*; 'The American Takes a Holiday,' and 'The American Credo,' through the courtesy of the *Forum*; 'Town and Suburb,' through the courtesy of the *Yale Review*; 'The Pleasure of Possession,' through the courtesy of the *Commonweal*. 'Peace and the Pacifist' has not appeared before in print.

Contents

TIMES AND TENDENCIES

. .

Town and Suburb

I prize civilization, being bred in towns, and liking to hear and see what new things people are up to. — GEORGE SANTAYANA.

WHEN I was a child, and people lived in towns and read poetry about the country, American cities had sharply accentuated characteristics, which they sometimes pretended to disparage, but of which they were secretly and inordinately proud. Less rich in tradition and inheritance than the beautiful cities of Europe, they nevertheless possessed historic backgrounds which coloured their communal life, and lent significance to social intercourse. The casual allusion of the Bostonian to his 'Puritan conscience,' the casual allusion of the Philadelphian to his 'Quaker forbears,' did not perhaps imply what they were meant to imply; but they indicated an outlook, and established an understanding. The nearness of friends in those days, the familiar, unchanging streets, the convivial clubs, the constant companionship helped to knit the strands of life into a close and well-defined pattern. Townsmen who made part of

this pattern were sometimes complacent without
much cause, and combative without any cause at
all; but the kind of cynicism which breeds fatigue
about human affairs was no part of their robust
constitutions.

A vast deal of abuse has been levelled against
cities; and the splendour of the parts they have
played has been dimmed by a too persistent
contemplation of their sins and their suffering.
Thomas Jefferson said that they were a sore on
the body politic; but then Jefferson appears to
have believed that farming was the only sinless
employment for man. When he found himself
loving Paris, because he was an American and
could not help it, he excused his weakness by re-
flecting that, after all, France was not England,
and by admitting a little ruefully that in Paris
'a man might pass his life without encountering a
single rudeness.' It was Jefferson's contemporary,
Cobbett, who, more than a hundred years ago,
started the denouncement of towns and town life
which has come rumbling down to us through the
century. London was the object of his supreme
detestation. Jews and Quakers lived in London
(so he said), also readers of the *Edinburgh Review*; and Jews, Quakers, and readers of the
Edinburgh Review were alike to him anathema.
'Cobbett,' mused Hazlitt, 'had no comfort in
fixed principles'; and for persistent fixity of

principles the *Review* ran a close third to the followers of Moses and of Fox.

It was pure wrong-headedness on the part of a proletarian fighting the cause of the proletariat to turn aside from the age-old spectacle of the townsman cradling his liberty, and rejoicing in his labour. There was not an untidy little mediæval city in Europe that did not help to carry humanity on its way. The artisans scorned by Froissart, the 'weavers, fullers, and other ill-intentioned people of the town,' who gave so much trouble to their betters, battled unceasingly for communal rights, and very often got them. The guilds, proud, quarrelsome and defiant, gave to the world the pride and glory of good work, and the pride and glory of freedom. As for London, those 'mettlesome Thames dwellers' held their own for centuries against every form of aggression. The silken cord which halts each king of England at Temple Bar on his way to coronation is a reminder of the ancient liberties of London. There stood the city's gates, which were opened only at the city's will. Charles the First signed his own death warrant when he undertook to coerce that stubborn will. When George the First asked Sir Robert Walpole how much it would cost to enclose Saint James's Park (long the delight of Londoners), and make it the private pleasure-ground of the king, the minister answered in four

words, 'Only three crowns, Sire,' and the Han-
overian shrugged his shoulders in silent understanding. What a strange people he had come to
rule!

We Americans think that we put up a brave
fight against the stupid obstinacy of George the
Third, and so we did for seven years. But London fought him all the years of his reign. 'It
was not for nothing,' says Trevelyan, 'that
Londoners with their compact organization, and
their habits of political discipline, proudly regarded themselves as the regular army of freedom.' George, whose conception of kingship
was singularly simple and primitive, regarded his
hostile city pretty much as Victoria regarded her
House of Commons. 'Very unmanageable and
troublesome,' was her nursery-governess's comment upon a body of men who were (though she
did not like to think so) the law-makers of
Britain.

With all history to contradict us, it is hardly
worth while to speak of city life as entailing
'spiritual loss,' because it is out of touch with
Nature. It is in touch with humanity, and humanity is Nature's heaviest asset. Blake, for
some reason which he never made plain (making
things plain was not his long suit), considered
Nature — 'the vegetable universe,' he phrased
it — to be depraved. He also considered Words-

worth to be more or less depraved because of his too exclusive worship at her shrine. 'I fear Wordsworth loves Nature,' he wrote (proud of his penetration) to Crabbe Robinson; 'and Nature is the work of the Devil. The Devil is in us all so far as we are natural.' Yet, when Wordsworth the Nature-lover stood on Westminster Bridge at dawn, and looked upon the sleeping London, he wrote a noble sonnet to her beauty:

Earth has not anything to show more fair.

When Blake looked upon London, he saw only her sorrow and her sin, he heard only 'the youthful harlot's curse' blighting her chartered streets. She was a trifle more depraved than Nature.

The present quarrel is not even between Nature and man, between the town and the country. It is between the town and the suburb, that midway habitation which fringes every American city, and which is imposing or squalid according to the incomes of suburbanites. This semi-rural life, though it has received a tremendous impetus in the present century, is not precisely new. Clerkenwell, London's oldest suburb, dates from the Plantagenets. John Stow, writing in the days of Elizabeth, says that rich men who dwelt in London town spent their money on hospitals for the sick and almshouses for the poor; but that rich men who dwelt in Shoreditch and other suburbs spent their money on costly residences to gratify their vanity. Being an antiquarian, and a freeman of Merchant Taylors' Company, Stow naturally held by the town.

It is the all-prevailing motor which stands responsible for the vast increase of suburban life in the United States, just as it was the coming of the locomotive which stood responsible for the increased population of London in Cobbett's last days. 'The facilities which now exist for moving human bodies from place to place,' he wrote in 1827 (being then more distressed by the excellence of the coaching roads than by the invasion of steam), 'are among the curses of the country, the destroyers of industry, of morals, and of happiness.'

It sounds sour to people who are now being taught that to get about easily and quickly is ever and always a blessing. The motor, we are given to understand, is of inestimable service because it enables men and women to do their work in the city, and escape with ease and comfort to their country homes — pure air, green grass, and so on. Less stress is laid upon the fact that it is also the motor which has driven many of these men and women into the suburbs by rendering the city insupportable; by turning into an open-air Bedlam streets which were once peaceful, comely and secure. Mr. Henry Ford, who has added the trying rôle of prophet to his other avocations, proclaimed six years ago that American cities were doomed. They had had their day. They had abused their opportunities. They had become unbearably expensive. They had grown so congested that his cars could make no headway in their streets. Therefore they must go. 'Delenda est Carthago; dum Ford deliberat.'

If Dickens still has readers as well as buyers, they must be grimly diverted by the art with which, in 'A Tale of Two Cities,' he works up the incident of the child run over and killed in the crowded streets of Paris. He makes this incident the key to all that follows. It justifies the murder by which it is avenged. It interprets the many murders that are on their way. It is an indictment of a class condemned to destruction for its wantonness. And to emphasize the dreadfulness of the deed, Dickens adds this damnatory sentence: 'Carriages were often known to drive on, and leave their wounded behind them.'

All this fire and fury over a child killed in the streets! Why, we Americans behold a yearly holocaust of children that would have glutted the bowels of Moloch. When thirty-two thousand people are slain by motors in twelve months, it is inevitable that a fair proportion of the dead should be little creatures too feeble and foolish to save themselves. As for driving on and leaving the wounded, that is a matter of such common occurrence that we have with our usual ingenuity invented a neat and expressive phrase for it, thus fitting it into the order of the day. The too-familiar headlines in the press, 'Hit-and-run victim found unconscious in the street,' 'Hit-and-run victim dies in hospital,' tell over and over again their story of callous cruelty. That such cruelty springs from fear is no palliation of the crime. Cowardice explains, but does not excuse, the most appalling brutalities. This particular form of ruffianism wins out (more's the pity!) in a majority of cases, and so it is likely to continue. In the year 1926, three hundred and sixty-one hit-and-run drivers remained unidentified, and escaped the penalty they deserved. Philippe de Comines cynically observed that he had known very few people who were clever enough to run away in time. The hit-and-runners of America could have given him points in this ignoble game.

The supposed blessedness of country life (see every anthology in the libraries) has been kindly extended to the suburbs. They are open to Whistler's objection that trees grow in them, and to Horace Walpole's objection that neighbours grow in them also. Rich men multiply their trees; poor men put up with the multiplication of neighbours. Rich men can conquer circumstances wherever they are. Poor men (and by this I mean men who are urbanely alluded to as in 'moderate circumstances') do a deal of whistling to keep themselves warm. They talk with serious fervour about Nature, when the whole of their landed estate is less than one of the back yards in which the town dwellers of my youth grew giant rosebushes that bloomed brilliantly in the mild city air. Mowing a grass-plot is to them equivalent to ploughing the soil. Sometimes they have not even a plot to mow, not even the shelter of a porch, nor the dignity and distinction of their own front door; but live in gigantic suburban apartment houses, a whole community under one roof like a Bornean village. Yet this monstrous standardization leaves them happy in the belief that they are country dwellers, lovers of the open, and spiritual descendants of the pioneers.

And the city? The abandoned city whose sons have fled to suburbs, what is it but a chaotic jumble of skyscrapers, public institutions, and parked cars? A transition stage is an uncomely stage, and cities on the move have a melancholy air of degradation. Shops elbow their uneasy way, business soars up into the air, houses disappear from their familiar settings, tired men and women drop into their clubs on the twentieth story of an inhospitable building, streets are dug up, paved, and dug up again, apparently with a view to buried treasure; dirt, confusion, and piercing noise are permitted by citizens who find it easier to escape such evils than to control them. An impression prevails that museums, libraries, and imposing banks constitute what our American press delights in calling 'the city beautiful.' That there is no beauty without distinction, and that distinction is made or marred by the constant, not the casual, contact of humanity, is a truth impressed upon our minds by countless towns in Europe, and by a great many towns in the United States. They tell their tale as plainly as a printed page, and far more convincingly.

If this tale is at an end; if the city has nothing to give but dirt, disorder, and inhuman racket, then let its sons fly to the suburbs and mow their grass-plots in content. If it has no longer a vehement communal life, if it is not, as it once was, the centre of pleasure and of purpose, if it is a thoroughfare and nothing else, then let them pass through it and escape. One thing is sure. No rural community, no suburban community, can ever possess the distinctive qualities that city dwellers have for centuries given to the world. The common interests, the keen and animated intercourse with its exchange of disputable convictions, the cherished friendships and hostilities — these things shaped townsmen into a compact, intimate society which left its impress upon each

successive generation. The home gives character
to the city; the man gives character to the home.
If, when his day's work is over, he goes speeding
off to a suburb, he breaks the link which binds
him to his kind. He says that he has good and
beautiful and health-giving relations with Nature — a tabloid Nature suited to his circumstances; but his relations with men are devitalized. Will Rogers indicated delicately this de-
vitalization when he said: 'League of Nations!
No, Americans aren't bothering about the League
of Nations. What they want is some place to
park their cars.'

Londoners, who have no cause to fear a semi-
deserted London, grieve that even a single
thoroughfare should change its aspect, should
lose its old and rich association with humanity.
So Mr. Street grieved over an altered Piccadilly,
reconstructing the dramas it had witnessed, the
history in which it had borne a part; wandering
in fancy from house to house, where dwelt the
great, the gay, and the undaunted. His book, he
said, was an epitaph. Piccadilly still lived, and
gave every day a clamorous demonstration of
activity; but her two hundred years of social
prominence were over, and her very distinguished
ghosts would never have any successors.

This is what is known as progress, and from it
the great cities of Europe have little or nothing to

fear. London, Paris, and Rome remain august arbiters of fate. They may lose one set of associations, but it would take centuries to rob them of all. Only a mental revolution could persuade their inhabitants that they are not good places to live in; and the eloquence of an archangel would be powerless to convince men bred amid arresting traditions that they are less fit to control the destinies of a nation than are their bucolic neighbours.

It would be hard to say when or why the American mind acquired the conviction that the lonely farmhouse or the sacrosanct village was the proper breeding-place for great Americans. It can hardly be due to the fact that Washington was a gentleman farmer, and Lincoln a country boy. These circumstances are without significance. The youthful Washington would have taken as naturally to fighting, and the youthful Lincoln to politics, if they had been born in Richmond and Louisville. But the notion holds good. It has been upheld by so keen an observer and commentator as Mr. Walter Lippmann, who has admitted that ex-Governor Smith, for whom he cherishes a profound and intelligent admiration, was debarred from the presidency by 'the accident of birth.' The opposition to him was based upon a sentiment 'as authentic and as poignant as his support. It was inspired by the feeling that the clamorous life of the city should not be acknowledged as the American ideal.'

This is, to say the least, bewildering. The qualities which Mr. Lippmann endorses in Mr. Smith, his 'sure instinct for realities,' his 'supremely good-humoured intelligence, and practical imagination about the ordinary run of affairs,' are products of his environment. His name can be written in the book of state as one who knows his fellow men; and he knows them because he has rubbed elbows with them from boyhood. The American people, says Mr. Lippmann, resent this first-hand knowledge. They will not condone or sanction it. 'In spite of the mania for size and the delusions of grandeur which are known as progress, there is still an attachment to village life. The cities exist, but they are felt to be alien; and in this uncertainty men turn to the scenes from which the leaders they have always trusted have come. The farmhouse at Plymouth, with old Colonel Coolidge doing the chores, was an inestimable part of President Coolidge's strength. The older Americans feel that it is in such a place that American virtue is bred; a cool, calm, shrewd virtue, with none of the red sins of the sidewalks of New York.'

There may be Americans who entertain this notion, but Mr. Lippmann, I am sure, is not of the number. He is well aware that sin does not belong to sidewalks. It has no predisposition towards pavements or mud roads. It is indigenous to man. Our first parents lived in the country, and they promptly committed the only sin they were given a chance to commit. Cain was brought up in the heart of the country, and he killed one of the small group of people upon whom he could lay his hands. That 'great cities, with their violent contrasts of riches and poverty, have produced class hatred all the world over,' is true — but a half-truth. The *Jacquerie*, most hideous illustration of well-earned class hatred, was a product of the countryside. So was the German *Bundschuh*. The French and the Russian Revolutionists lighted up wide landscapes with burning homes, and soaked the innocent soil with blood. The records of crime prove the universality of crime. Bastards and morons and paranoiacs and degenerates and the criminally insane may be found far from the sidewalks of New York.

To live in stable harmony with Nature should be as easy for the town dweller as for the countryman. As a matter of fact, it should be easier, inasmuch as 'the brutal, innocent injustice of Nature' leaves the town dweller little the worse. Like authorship, Nature is a good stick but a bad crutch, and they love her best who are not dependent on her caprices:

Town and Suburb

Bred in the town am I,
So would I wish to be,
Loving its glimpses of sky,
Swayed by its human sea.

If Browning in his incomparable poem, 'Up at a
Villa — Down in the City,' appears to mock at
the street-loving lady, he nevertheless makes out
a strong case in her favour. I have sympathized
with her all my life; and it is worthy of note that
the poet himself preferred to live in towns, and,
like Santayana, see what people were up to. The
exceptionally fortunate man was Montaigne who
drew a threefold wisdom from the turbulent city
of Bordeaux, which he ruled as mayor; from the
distinction of Paris and the French court, where
he was a gentleman of the king's chamber; and
from the deep solitude of Auvergne, where stood
his ancestral home. He knew the life of the politician, the life of the courtier, the life of the farmer.
Therefore, being kindly disposed towards all the
vanities of the world, he was balanced and moderate beyond the men of his day.

Lovers of the town have been content, for the
most part, to say they loved it. They do not brag
about its uplifting qualities. They have none of
the infernal smugness which makes the lover of
the country insupportable. 'I gravitate to a
capital by a primary law of nature,' said Henry
Adams, and was content to say no more. It

did not seem to occur to him that the circumstance called for ardour or for apology. But when Mr. John Erskine turns his ungrateful back upon the city which loves him, he grows enthusiastic over the joy of regaining 'the feel of the soil, the smell of earth and rain, the dramatic contact of the seasons, the companionship of the elements.' It is a high note to strike; but if for drama we must fall back upon the seasons, and for companionship upon the elements, ours will be a dreary existence in a world which we have always deemed both dramatic and companionable. If, as Mr. Erskine asserts, spring, summer, autumn, and winter are 'annihilated' in town, we lose their best, but we escape their worst, features. That harsh old axiom, 'Nature hates a farmer,' has a fund of experience behind it. A distinguished surgeon, having bought, in a Nature-loving mood, a really beautiful farm, asked an enlightened friend and neighbour: 'What had I better do with my land?' To which the answer came with judicious speed: 'Pave it.'

There is a vast deal of make-believe in the carefully nurtured sentiment for country life, and the barefoot boy, and the mountain girl. I saw recently in an illustrated paper a picture of a particularly sordid slum in New York's unredeemed East Side, and beneath it the reproachful query: 'Is this a place to breed supermen?' Assuredly not. Neither is a poverty-stricken, fallen-to-pieces farmhouse, with a hole in its screen door; or a grim little home in a grim little suburb, destitute of beauty and cheer. If we want super-men (and to say the truth Germany has put us out of conceit with the species), we shall have to breed them under concentrated violet rays. Sunshine and cloud refuse to sponsor the race.

When Dr. Johnson said, 'The man who is tired of London is tired of life,' he expressed only his own virile joy in humanity. When Lamb said, 'That man must have a rare receipt for melancholy who can be dull in Fleet Street,' he summed up the brimming delight afforded him by this epitome of civilization. When Sydney Smith wrote from the dignified seclusion of his rectory at Combe-Florey, 'I look forward eagerly to the return of the bad weather, coal fires, and good society in a crowded city,' he put the pleasures of the mind above the pleasures of the senses. All these preferences are temperately and modestly stated. It was only when Lamb was banished from the thronged streets he loved that he grew petulant in his misery. It was only when he dreamed he was in Fleet Market, and woke to the torturing dulness of Enfield, that he cried out: 'Give me old London at fire and plague times rather than this healthy air, these tepid gales, these purposeless exercises.' Yet even then he claimed no moral superiority over the Nature-lovers who were beginning to make themselves heard in England. He knew only that London warmed his sad heart, and that it broke when he lost her.

Generally speaking, and leaving out of consideration the very poor to whom no choice in life is given, men and women who live in cities or in suburbs do so because they want to. Men and women who live in small towns do so because of their avocations, or for other practical reasons. They are right in affirming that they like it. I once said to a New York taxi-driver: 'I want to go to Brooklyn.' To which he made answer: 'You mean you have to.' So with the small-town dwellers. They may or may not 'want to,' but the 'have to' is sure. Professional men, doctors and dentists especially, delight in living in the suburbs, so that those who need their services cannot reach them. The doctor escapes from his patients, who may fall ill on Saturday, and die on Sunday, without troubling him. The dentist is happy in that he can play golf all Saturday and Sunday while his patients agonize in town. Only the undertaker, man's final servitor, stands staunchly by his guns.

It is not because the city is big, but because it draws to its heart all things that are gay and keen, that life in its streets is exhilarating. It is short of birds (even the friendly little sparrows are being killed off by the drip of oil into its gutters); but that is a matter of more concern to the city's cats than to the city's inhabitants. It is needlessly noisy; but the suburb is not without its sufferings on this score. Motors shriek defiance in the leafy lanes, dogs bark their refrain through the night, and the strange blended sounds of the radios, like lost souls wailing their perdition, float from piazza to piazza. These are remediable evils; but so are most of the city's evils, which are not remedied because Americans are born temporizers, who dislike nothing so much as abating a public nuisance. They will spend time and money on programmes to outlaw war, because that is a purely speculative process; but they will not stir themselves to outlaw excessive noise or dangerous speeding, because such measures mean actual campaigning. 'The city,' says one clear-eyed and very courageous American, 'is the flower of civilization. It gives to men the means to make their lives expressive. It offers a field of battle, and it could be made a livable place if its sons would stay and fight for it, instead of running away.'

Peace and the Pacifist

NOW that the world is at peace (excepting only China, and India, and Afghanistan, and possibly a South American Republic or two that cannot be betted on with security, and some strips of country policed by American marines whose activities are not officially recognized as fighting) — now, I repeat, that the rest of the world is at peace, and ardently desires to remain so, it is time that pacifists reduced their sentimentalities to order. There are few things that cannot be injured by intemperate zeal, and goodwill has never been one of them. It is a plant of slow, not to say sluggish, growth, unlikely to be forced into bloom by gusts of artificial enthusiasm. 'Most fervently do I wish in the interests of peace that there were fewer discussions about the methods of perpetuating peace,' says Mr. Sisley Huddleston. Yet discussions about methods represent an approach to the practical. They are sane by comparison with 'Peace Pilgrims' marching through a country which desires only to be left in peace, or Peace Societies denouncing the 'blood-thirsty timidity' (a curious phrase) of supposititious militarists, or Peace Education which involves the eliminat-

ing from history of all that is definitely historical.

Nothing can make the men and women who
lived as adults through the World War consent to
witness another. The protracted pain of those
four years is an ever-present memory; and there
are many of us who have failed to regain the light-
ness of heart which seemed a normal condition
before this horror came. It lasted so long, it was
so inescapable, it was so pitiful and so malign.
Not only did we see in our mind's eye day after
weary day the flaming villages of France, her
shattered cathedrals, and ruined countryside;
but we visioned other sufferings hitherto unknown.
The poison gas, with Raemaeker's terrible cartoon
to show us what it meant; the fifteen thousand
non-combatants drowned at sea; the little dead
children lying in rows on the Irish coast after
the sinking of the Lusitania. Who could bear a
repetition of such things, and live? Yet we are
told that the workshops and laboratories of the
world are preparing weapons of destruction more
terrible than any known fifteen years ago. We
sink — after months of argument — a few mid-
dle-aged ships which might have been permitted
to live out their lives in tranquillity; but airplane
bombs which can precipitate upon a doomed city
two tons of T.N.T., and phosphorus bombs carrying their acid fire, make cruisers and so-called

destroyers seem like old-fashioned and genial things. We can forbid a nation to mobilize an army or float a battleship; but we cannot prevent thoughtful scientists from perfecting instruments of slaughter compared with which Attila's methods of warfare were restricted, gentlemanly, and creditable.

There will not be another war while the people who remember the four terrible years can legislate for peace; but it must be borne in mind that a new generation has grown up since Armistice Day; and that while in Europe it still suffers the consequences of those four years, it is everywhere free from recollections. This generation knows little of what really happened (war plays and moving pictures cannot be regarded as sources of information), and much of its ignorance is due to an impression on our part that the road to peace lies in forgetfulness. We are purposed not to offend, and it is hard to discuss any episode of history (let alone a world war) without offending somebody. So we have softened edges in the interests of harmony, and have summoned all the resources of sentiment to keep them definitely blurred.

In this consideration for the erring we place an unwise trust. The League of Nations is striving to make war difficult, the World Court and the Kellogg Pact propose to make it illegal.

Back of such serious endeavours must lie the will of the people. Dean Inge told Americans five years ago that it was their duty to prevent another war. He did not say precisely why, and he did not say precisely how; but there was a flattering import in his words. About the same time, Mr. Houghton, representing the United States, told London that if Europe did not keep the peace, his country would lend no more money. He spoke as the typical creditor addressing the typical debtor, and his countrymen at home said that it was a sound business talk. Their sense of importance was gratified, and the purely negative character of this olive branch was in accord with their cherished aloofness. That Europe is committed to anxiety does not seem to have occurred to them; her desperate desire for peace, as evinced by the Geneva Protocol and the Locarno Pact, is not sufficiently clear to us today.

Perhaps this is because reasonable fears create unreasonable misgivings. Every nation is convinced that she is dedicated to peace; but that the actions of other nations are open to suspicion. Every system of government is warranted by its upholders to insure harmonious relations, while every other system must lead inevitably to war. The Fascist believes and says that when a strong man armed keepeth his court, those things which he possesseth are in peace. More liberal commonwealths predict year after year the civil strife which will throw Fascism into the discard, and make its leaders helpless to face an adversary. English and American newspapers have long told us that Russia is menaced by enemies on her frontier, and by the revolt of her ill-used peasantry. Russia, as interpreted by Stalin, has now come forward to say that capitalist nations are 'drifting surely to war,' because it is the nature of capital to prey upon the weak, and quarrel over the booty. In proposing universal and complete disarmament, the Soviet State made a gesture so sweeping and imperative that an uneasy world felt more uneasy than ever, wondering what on earth she was up to. We have the assurance of M. Henri Barbusse that her only motive was the finding of 'ways and means to strengthen peace and eliminate the danger of war between the nations'; but in her overtures to 'the toiling, oppressed, and exhausted peoples of Europe' there were allusions to the overthrow of 'existing capitalist governments' that were not calculated to insure confidence. Their ultimate goal was peace; but they sounded like 'war to end war,' a phrase that familiarity has failed to endear.

Meanwhile, American pacifists are casting discredit upon patriotism as illiberal and militant. They seek to wean school-children from uncon-

sidered loyalty to the flag, and from enthusiasm
— based largely upon fireworks — for the Fourth
of July. They denounce military drill in schools
and colleges, branding this harmless exercise 'as
a positive suggestion of the hatred which is evidenced in warfare.' Yet it seems unlikely that
young men who have been taught to march in
line, and to handle firearms without blowing
themselves to pieces, should be inspired thereby
to hate their fellow creatures. One wonders how
many of the gangsters and gunmen who terrorize
our communities acquired their skill in camps;
and whether the merry game of banditry might
not lose its zest if honest men were better prepared to defend themselves and their property.
No American can boast that his life is safe in
any American town. Bands of earnest youths
vow that they will never lift their hands to save
their country from assault, while bands of equally
earnest thugs, who take no vows, keep their
fingers perpetually on the trigger.

Intensive propaganda in the interests of pacifism denies the purposes, the accomplishments,
and the intrepidities of war. Its hero is the conscientious objector, its martyr is the interned
alien. Heartrending fiction has been written about
these ill-used men, and the only soldiers who can
rival them in popular esteem are those who come
home seared and disillusioned, with a settled dis-

belief in humanity, and a 'now it can be told' expression in their sombre eyes. For a dozen years after Armistice Day the war was the acknowledged scapegoat for every shortcoming. The inordinate desire of women to take their clothes off ('if it were not for the police,' said a Philadelphia judge, 'you couldn't keep clothes on a lady'), the easy prevalence of something which the Scriptures call adultery, the arrogant and unabashed lawlessness of the criminally inclined, these phenomena were ascribed directly to four years of combat. One cannot help feeling sorry for those stupid mediæval sinners who did heavy penance for their own sins, when they were never without a war of sorts upon which they could have saddled the blame.

England, always impatient with crime, put a speedy end to robbery and violence, which disappeared, leaving behind them a comet-like trail of detective stories. One of these that fell my way told with adorable simplicity the tale of a high-souled, nobly endowed gentleman, who was so blighted by his experience in the trenches (from which he emerged sound in body though warped in soul) that he became a master thief. Having no need of money and a nice taste in curios, he stole only rare objects of art, and found himself the possessor of a well-chosen and inexpensively acquired collection. Now, when the heroine, who

possessed every virtue and every grace, discovered that the man she hoped to marry was a
thief, did she find anything to regret or censure
in his conduct? Not for a moment! Rendered
clear-sighted by pacifism and by love, she recognized at once where lay the responsibility, and
cried, in just and poignant anger, 'Damn the
war!'

It sounds too absurd for notice; but the same
spirit which made possible the printing of this
engaging nonsense made possible the printing of
the narrative called 'The Deserter,' in the *Atlantic Monthly* for September, 1930. It told a
very common experience with a somewhat un-
common candour. There have always been de-
serters from the ranks of war, and always for the
same reason. 'I ran away from my wife because
she was going to have a baby,' said a young mu-
latto to me, 'and I ran away from the navy because it was worse than being married.' Colonel
Isaac Jones Wistar, who has told us with a good
deal of vivacity his experiences in raising a Pennsylvania regiment in the first year of the Civil
War, says that if the men enlisted when they
were drunk, they deserted when they were sober;
and that if they enlisted when they were sober,
they deserted when they were drunk. He would
get them safely on a train bound for headquarters
in New York; and after it had started they would

jump off, 'with a courage worthy of a better cause, and were left scattered promiscuously in a wide swath across the State of New Jersey.' It never occurred to these venturesome slackers to write their experiences, which would not at that time have made popular reading; but the 'Memoirs of a Bounty-Jumper' might have been as thrilling as the memoirs of a general. He certainly ran a heavier risk of being shot.

The *Atlantic Monthly* 'Deserter' had an easier time of it. Being out of conceit with his job in a clothing shop in London, he was not unwilling, when 'called up,' to try his luck in France. The only mishap he encountered there was due to his own carelessness in standing too close to a car from which lumber was being unloaded. The only hardship of which he makes mention was the 'uncomfortable army bed'; but then nobody does like an uncomfortable bed. The possibility of being killed was, however, disagreeably present in his mind, and helped him to the conclusion that the war was 'futile.' Therefore he decided to run away from it, than which nothing appears to have been easier. Being sent home on leave, he gave a Dublin instead of a London address, went un-molested to Ireland, was welcomed by the Sinn Feiners who were not particular about their com-pany, and was consulted by a young woman with 'a beautiful Irish voice' as to the feasibility of poisoning the British Cabinet, which sounds like Birmingham at his funniest. After the Armistice he returned to England, and got a better job on the strength of his regimental cap badge, which he had astutely preserved to serve him in such an emergency.

There is nothing remarkable in this ignoble narrative save the fact that it was written, printed, and presumably read. There has been little heretofore that men have not been willing to tell us about themselves. Now we know that there is nothing. The 'Deserter' belongs to a recognizable type which can be multiplied by the hundred. It is commonly compared to an unloved little animal of the woods, which is, I think, deeply wronged by the comparison. Emerson might perhaps have refused to acknowledge it as human; but Emerson managed to live and die believing in the dignity of man. The thing to understand is that it was possible to publish the adventure in the pages of the *Atlantic Monthly* because pacifism stands committed to the belief that war is in itself, and apart from controlling circumstances, reprehensible. This paves the way to what is called a 'common-sense view,' which is 'safety first,' with no other instinct or sentiment to intervene.

The plays and moving pictures that betrayed themselves too openly as propaganda followed the same line of reasoning. They showed the needless waste of war with no concern for its cause, and no sympathy for its heroisms. The only play innocent of purpose (save, indeed, the age-old purpose of showing the reaction of men to circumstance, which has been the animating motive of drama since its earliest incipience) was *What Price Glory*. It was a coarse and blasphemous production with one scene of surpassing tenderness. It dealt with a low grade of humanity, and it closed on a high note, the call to duty which differentiates man from beast. Thousands saw it, and were, I think, the better for the seeing, though it was not designed for their edification.

Its successor in the field, *Journey's End*, and the war films that followed were sermons, sermons admirably delivered, but with the text always in evidence. The drunkenness of Stanhope in *Journey's End* was not merely induced by life in the trenches, it was its inevitable consequence. The tragedy in the third act was brought about by the callous indifference of the British commanding officer who sacrificed his men's lives for a piece of worthless information; just as the hecatomb of deaths in the American film, *The Big Parade*, was caused by the arrogant conceit of the American captain who refused to dig in when warned of an ambush. The point driven home was the general unworthiness of the country and the cause for which men die, the disillusionment which is bound to follow what was once thought a noble emotion. 'Among the enlightened from Goethe's time to our own,' writes Mr. Ludwig Lewisholm with tearful solemnity, 'exclusive patriotism has never been thought of as anything but a menace and a shame.' It is hard lines on Goethe to saddle him with the responsibility for our slackness. He was not much of a citizen, but he was a very great poet. And he expressed a modest hope that men, young men especially, who read his poetry might be stimulated thereby to endeavour.

Perhaps the Americans, all under thirty, who day after day besieged the consulates of the Brazilian Government, seeking a chance to fight the revolutionists (about whom they had little knowledge, and against whom they bore no grudge), were the fair fruits of internationalism. If we are to love all countries as our own, why not seek a bit of adventure in the ranks of any one of them? Only patient and reiterated assertions that Brazil had no foreign legionaries and desired none kept these soldiers of fortune in their own happy and peaceful land.

A year or two ago a little French town (not too small to have lost three hundred sons in the World War) was celebrating the Fourteenth of July. The schoolmistress who trained the children to sing at the celebration conceived the happy thought of changing the words of the 'Marseillaise' to express a universal goodwill, somewhat out of keeping with its original significance. But no sooner had the young innocents started the opening lines,

Allons enfants de toutes les patries,

when the townspeople shouted their disapproval and wrath. Not for a moment would they tolerate an innovation which they considered both sacrilegious and illogical; sacrilegious because it profaned a tradition, illogical because Rouget de Lisle was not inspired by love of England to write the 'Marseillaise,' and the Bastile had not been destroyed in the interests of Austria and Spain.

Did this imply that the little French town stood ready to risk her remaining sons in another war, or that she mistrusted sentiment as a foundation for security? She would not pretend that she cherished the glory of Italy as she cherished her own, or that the fields of Silesia were as dear to her as the fields of Morbihan or the Côte d'Or. No one would have believed her if she had. In that veracious book, 'French France,' the author, Mr. Oliver Madox Hueffer, tells us that a little French girl to whom he had grown attached informed him one afternoon that she did not like him any longer because he was English, and she had just learned in school that the English had burned Jeanne d'Arc. It seemed to him an insufficient reason for breaking off amicable relations; and he lamented to a Frenchwoman of his acquaintance the tendency of schoolbooks to foster a spirit of animosity in children's hearts rather than a spirit of brotherly love. His friend objected, though with placidity, to the use of the word 'love' in this connection. She did not feel it, and she did not see any need to feel it. She said that she wished England well, and that she believed a strong and prosperous England would be to the advantage of France. But it seemed to her that both nations could make their way in the world without unreal and unnecessary protestations of affection.

The French mind is a rational mind. Fervency is but a wisp of straw in binding states together; but the economic advantages of peace could be pressed home if all governments would consent to act with fundamental decency in international relations. We do not owe the duty to other countries that we owe to our own; but a hard indifference to their interests is not the shrewd business principle that we are apt to think it. 'An essentially selfish nation,' says Mr. Reinhold Niebuhr, 'cannot afford to be trusting. Its selfishness destroys the redemptive and morally creative power of its trust.'

That the peace of fact is not the peace of principle is a bitter truth established long ago. To assail Christianity and civilization because of this truth is satisfactory only to the assailants. Christianity is a counsel of perfection, and the civilizations of the world are admittedly — because inevitably — imperfect. Permanent peace would involve inconceivable changes in political economy. We need hardly pause to consider them, when even the vision of an internationalized market lies far beyond our ken. In every formula presented for our consideration the element of self-sacrifice is conspicuously lacking. There are reformers like Mr. Borah who would deal with war as with alcohol, and with probably the same results. There are reformers who frame pacts and treaties which are without adequate ways and means to compel the signatories to keep their word. There are reformers who put their faith in a boundless and baseless goodwill. But there are no reformers who propose that all countries including their own, and that all men including themselves, should sacrifice self-interest in the interests of the world at large. If there were any such, they would be without adherents. The cost would be too great. 'We cannot,' says Santayana, 'at this immense distance from a rational social order, judge what concessions individual genius would be called upon to

make in a system of education and government
in which all attainable good should be scientif-
ically pursued.'

The New Republic says that the United States
is a belligerent country. Assuredly not! Bullying, perhaps, but not belligerent. The Civil
War was fought in anguish of spirit. The Spanish War hardly rose to the level of belligerency.
No one can say that we wanted to fight in the
World War. We held back as long as it was humanly possible to do so. We elected a president
because he had kept us out of it. If the safety of
American ships and the lives of American citizens
could have been reasonably assured without our
fighting for them, we never should have fought.
Under similar provocation we should fight again
tomorrow. Fortunately a world, rendered cautious by experience, is not prepared to offer such
provocation.

The misuse of words is too common to provoke
attention. An illuminated text in a shop-window
which stated 'The New Patriotism is Peace,'
gave satisfaction no doubt to a purchaser who
did not stop to consider that patriotism is a
sentiment, and peace is a possession. It would
have been as correct to say 'The New Kindness
is Prosperity,' or 'The New Piety is Good Health.'
The old heroic tags familiar to our schooldays,
'Dieu et mon Droit,' 'Fiat justicia ruat cælum,'

'Dulce et decorum est pro patria mori,' had a verbal accuracy, a fine sharp finish that made them easy and pleasant to remember. And, after all, patriotism in its original 'exclusive' sense is one of the three great animating principles that stand responsible for the history of mankind, the other two being religion and sexual love. I am told that religion is no longer a vital force, controlling the minds of civilized men, and thrusting them into action. If patriotism becomes an emotion too expansively benevolent to make men willing to live and die for something concrete like a king or a country, we shall have nothing left to fall back upon but sexual love, which is a strong individual urge, but lacks breadth and scope of purpose. It burned Troy; but it did not build Rome, or secure the Magna Charta, or frame the Constitution of the United States.

A nation-wide and popular error holds that the prevalence of war in history makes for militarism. Reformers are annoyed by the number of battles that have been fought, and by the handsome things that have been said about the men who won them. They believe that this praise dazzles the mind of youth. But every student knows that the wars of the world have darkened the face of the world. Every student sees the poverty and pain of the conquered and of the conquerors. History is not written in the

interests of morality. It has things to tell, and
it tells them. Generations of men have survived
the happenings and the telling, principally because they took short views of life. Mr. Stephen
Benét, in that notable book, 'John Brown's
Body,' has expressed to perfection the simple and
sane mentality which made men carry on, and
preserved the life of a nation:

When a war came along, you fought on your own proper
    side;
You didn't blast both sides with Mercutio's curse,
And hide in a wilderness.

Nevertheless, it takes all the truth, beauty and
spirit of the book to make possible its reading.
The four years of Civil War are not to be lightly
followed by one who knows what was implied in
Lincoln's last call for troops, and in Lee's last
stand.

It seemed hardly worth while for Mr. David
Jayne Hill to say that 'defensive armament is
not in itself a cause of war. It is a necessary
means of protection against hostile designs so
long as they may still exist. It sounded a little
like saying 'a defensive greatcoat is not in itself a
cause of cold weather. It is a necessary means of
protection against wintry winds so long as they
may still exist.' Yet this simple and obvious
truth met with angry denial from sentimentalists
who admit the dangers of a late spring, but who

refuse to believe that the world seethes with antagonisms. Russia, for example, impervious to framed texts, is frank in her hostility to her neighbours. Most of them are remote neighbours, for which they thank God; but all of them are tolerably aware that, with the barriers down, the great bear may still be the oyster king.

When Mr. Ford's peace ship sailed for Europe with Madame Schwimmer and Judge Lindsey (then just beginning his career of successful notoriety) to help its master 'get the men out of the trenches by Christmas,' we were too heavy-hearted to enjoy the absurdity of the situation. When the war was over, the episode was forgotten. When in 1915 a congress of women met at The Hague, they offered the admirable arguments in favour of peace which have been repeated at every subsequent conference. When some of the members visited the foreign offices and presented appeals, they were urbanely received, and the fighting went on. Miss Addams was indeed able to report a very gratifying 're-volt against war' on the part of young English-men and Germans whom she interviewed; but it made no dint in the contending ranks. Her assertion that the soldiers went into action drunk aroused a flurry of anger in the serious-minded, and some ribald jests concerning the relative value of brandy and beer as incentives to valour.

It was noticeable that no Frenchwomen took part in the congress, or in the subsequent activities. How could they with a German army of occupation in their land! An invaded country has scant dependence upon argument. France knew that peace in 1915 would mean for her the uttermost defeat.

Sixteen years have gone by, and the world is still busy considering the 'Cause and Cure of War'; still probing into the heart of human nature, still balancing the chances of self-sacrifice. Mr. Root spoke nobly and truly when he said that the World Court might fail of its avowed purpose; 'but God forbid that it should fail because America has refused to do her part.' America is prepared to do her part, fairly, squarely, and authoritatively, provided always that it implies no surrender of those advantages which we ascribe in some measure to the well-judged partiality of the Almighty, and in some measure to our active coöperation with his plans.

Mr. Philip Guedalla, whose charm as a historian lies in his happy detachment — for the time — from the prejudices of his own day, tells us in his life of Palmerston the story of a nameless British officer, who, dismounted and wounded in one of the battles of the Peninsula War, roared at his men: 'Fifty-Seventh, die hard!' It is an anecdote eminently fitted to arouse the ire and the ridicule of his readers. It is as remote from modernity as if it had happened on the field of Marathon. Why should those men, ill-fed, ill-paid, indomitable, have died hard? Why should they have died at all? What was the Peninsula War to them? Six years it lasted, and Wellington admitted a death-list of nearly thirty-six thousand (four thousand more lives lost than were extinguished by motors in the United States in 1930), while he was building up an army 'which could go anywhere and do anything.'

We have travelled far since then. We have grown lucid, and logical, and humane, and incompetent. 'Those active Islanders,' who kept even Napoleon on the jump, are now 'more than usual calm.' The recently published memoirs of a whilom Cambridge professor conclude with a glowing tribute to British social and political advancement; to the soberness of the people, the rectitude of the government, the 'awakened conscience' of the nation. And yet, and yet — the England whose simpleton sons, 'fools-to-free-the-world,' died hard on the blood-stained fields of Spain was an England growing greater and greater every year; a power directing, re-straining, and clarifying the turbulent life of Europe. The England of the 'Deserter' and the Dole is on another plane, and who shall predict the end?

Cure-Alls

IT WAS a chemist's window on a dingy street-corner, and there stood in it a portrait of the once famous practitioner whose sign was an uplifted forefinger, and whose slogan was 'While there is life, there is hope.' Beneath, printed in fair large text, was this jubilant couplet:

> There's a Munyon pill
> For every ill!

and, reading it, I was made pleasantly aware of the survival of human confidences: not merely the confidences of my childhood, but the confidences of the childhood of the world. For uncounted years mankind believed, ignorantly but not illogically, that Nature, who had provided multitudinous ills for her children, had also provided correspondingly multitudinous cures. The ills she gave open-handedly, mindful of her duty to destroy; the cures she gave grudgingly and under pressure, but they were always to be found for the seeking.

With a still more touching simplicity, we believe in this age of experience that for the evils, spiritual, material, and intellectual, which beset us, remedies are at hand. There's a pious pill, a social pill, a political pill, for every ill, and they are offered to us at the street-corners of life. Their action is assured. Their numbers are as remarkable as their variety. They range all the way from licensing parents, which is warranted to curtail the birth-rate, to a bonus on babies, which is warranted to increase it; from simplicity of living, which is doing without things we do not need, to 'consumptionism,' which is acquiring things we do not want; from Fundamentalism, which is the triumph of the rigid, to Spiritism, which is the triumph of the nebulous. Distinguished specialists offer us private and particular remedies for our private and particular ills. A few years ago an enterprising lady succeeded in persuading a number of Americans, who had heretofore been considered sane, that if they changed their proper names — she chose the new names — and wore specified colours — she chose the colours — they would grow as healthy, wealthy and wise as if they got up early in the morning.

Colour psychology is playing an interesting part in the rehabilitation of the world. The happy possessors of an aura distinguishable to the medium's eye are very particular about its shade. Readers of 'Raymond' — and a dozen years ago everybody was a reader of 'Raymond' — will remember the use of colours, as described in that jocund volume. According to reports received through 'Feda,' a youthful control of volatile disposition and retarded mentality, spirits residing in the 'beyond' absorbed goodness and greatness through rays of parti-coloured light. If they were unloving, they stood in pink rays and grew affectionate. If they were stupid, they stood in orange rays and grew intelligent. If they were materialistic, they stood in blue rays, the most delicate and powerful of all, blue being the light of pure spiritual healing. The simplicity of this device, compared to our cumbersome human methods, could not be too highly recommended; and we were assured that in the coming years the world would learn the curative and educational value of colours, and so be spared much misdirected effort.

Nine years before the revelations of 'Raymond,' Achille Ricciardi, an ingenious and enthusiastic theorist, assigned an æsthetic value to colours; and his assumptions are reset from time to time by equally ingenious and far more practical authorities. Ricciardi held that colours have a life of their own, 'a rich treasury of emotive connotations,' and that they not only feed our sensations but control them. He never affirmed that these emotive connotations were alike, under different conditions. The moral values of red and blue were the only ones he believed to be beyond dispute. Today we hear strange stories of rooms painted yellow in which nobody feels cold, and of rooms painted slate-blue in which nobody feels warm; of rooms hung in violet in which people weep without cause, and of rooms hung with orange in which people laugh without reason. One colour psychologist informs us that light brown and blue inspire confidence in business ventures, and that green walls and yellow curtains inspire corresponding confidence in religious teaching. Another, equally assured, is of the opinion that a pink kitchen will make a cook contented with her work, and so bring about the radical regeneration of the world.

It is all very interesting, very sanguine, and a little contradictory. From those mysterious statistics that are compiled by people who enjoy an infinity of leisure, and the precise purposes of which are hidden from the profane, we learn that yellow — the delight of the Orient — is regarded with disfavour by American undergraduates of both sexes. These young people can hardly have inherited the aversion of the early Christians for what was once considered a lascivious hue; but a large majority confess to liking it least among colours. Perhaps its arbitrary and wholly fanciful association with a certain type of journalism, as well as with slackers and obstructionists during the war, may lie at the root of this antipathy. I, at least, should be sorry to see it exchanged for

pink in American kitchens, were it only for the
sake of the child, Henry Adams, aged three, sitting in the sunlight on the yellow kitchen floor,
and remembering all the rest of his life this first
happy consciousness of colour.

Our grandfathers and our great grandfathers
were not without their panaceists, who were as
sanguine as folly could make them, but who
lacked the business acumen of their successors.
Most of Emerson's friends were engaged in making over a world which was a matter of such indifference to him. As he wisely said, he could get
along without it. Alcott had a baker's dozen of
cure-alls which ranged from dining without edible
food to farming without necessary implements,
the plough being a symbol of something evil —
nobody knew exactly what. The spade alone was
a pure and holy instrument which made up in
sanctity what it lacked in achievement. Then
there was the printer, Edward Taylor, who proposed to redeem society by abolishing money, a
thorough-going measure save in regard to himself and his followers who had none to abolish.
I have always fancied that I should have liked
those semi-religious reformers who called themselves 'Come-Outers.' Whatever it was you
were in, there was something bold and persuasive
in being invited to come out of it.

All these theorists worked on a scale so modest

as to be fantastic; but it must be conceded that they never hesitated to run counter to the partialities and prejudices of their time. Their reforms, however absurd, had at least one element of authenticity, they were unpalatable. Their successors developed sound business instincts; promising much, asking little, and pointing always in the direction that people wanted to go. When Mrs. Eddy conceived the brilliant idea of abolishing illness and pain, she had the sympathy of the world with her; and her cure-all was the most stupendous that civilized man had known. If at times she bore a curious resemblance to Owen Glendower (I mean Shakespeare's Glendower who could call spirits from the vasty deep), the practical and commercial side of her nature never lost control. It pleased her to believe that snow stopped falling at her command; but it was not by bullying the elements that she built up her giant following and her giant fortune. Nobody cared much whether the snow stopped or not. But to persuade a fat woman that 'obesity is an adipose belief in yourself as a substance,' was to save that fat woman from the daily misery of dieting. To bring a man 'out of a plaster cast into truth,' was to connive at his escape from surgery. What he escaped into was a matter of unconcern.

The cure-alls of the present day are infinitely

various and infinitely obliging. Applied psychology, autosuggestion, and royal roads to learning
or to wealth are urged upon us by kindly, if not
altogether disinterested, reformers. Simple and
easy systems for the dissolution of discord and
strife; simple and easy systems for the development of personality and power. Booklets of
counsel on 'How to Get What We Want,' which
is impossible; booklets on 'Visualization,' warranted to make us want what we get, which is
ignoble. 'Let science cure your ills!' is the
clarion cry of one miracle-monger. 'Let culture
crown your life!' is the soft whisper of another.
The common pursuit of wealth is proffered as a
human bond, which it has never been. The individual pursuit of knowledge is proffered as a
social asset, which it can never be.

When Dr. Eliot selected his famous five-foot
shelf of books, he little dreamed that it would be
lifted to the proud preëminence of a cure-all.
For years scholars and readers had diverted themselves by making lists of the best ten books, the
best fifty books, the best hundred books, the best
books to read on a desert island, presuming we
were cast away with a little library of our own
selection. Indeed, the Librarian of the University
of Pennsylvania came forward with a list of the
best thousand books, which was warranted to
keep us profitably employed for the rest of our

natural lives. Dr. Eliot was, however, the first to associate measurement with erudition; and the practical nature of this device, combined with the sanction of his name, gave to his list, which was frankly personal, ascendency over other lists, which were frankly scholastic or frankly popular. Literature is alien to the natural man; but the limitations of a five-foot shelf were everywhere understood and appreciated.

With what result! Dr. Eliot expressed from time to time a veritable enthusiasm for that shop-worn word, 'efficiency'; but it was never a factor in his intellectual pursuits, and it was certainly not haunting his mind when he compiled his brief and weighty list. One does not grow efficient by reading Jonson, or Shelley, or Marlowe. The irony of fate decreed that his five-foot shelf should, in the course of time, be converted into a five-foot pill-box, the contents of which, when absorbed in homœopathic doses, are warranted to fit us for all the emergencies of life. We are asked to believe that financiers are impressed with the conversation of young men who have read 'The Wealth of Nations,' and that pretty girls surrender themselves to the charm of suitors conversant with the 'Areopagitica.' 'The Fruits of Solitude' lends sparkle to a dinner party; the 'Religio Medici' and the 'Confessions' of Saint Augustine, books written for the secret pleasure and the secret solace of

humanity, assume an unsuspected value when re-
tailed for the enlightenment of society. Education, once defined as 'the transmission of a moral
and intellectual tradition,' has crystallized into a
compact substance, imparted without reserve
and absorbed without effort, as useful as a ready
reckoner, as universally popular as a trump card.

It would seem strange in any other age than
this, and in any other land than ours, to have
works of scholarship urged upon us — not as an
occupation for our own leisure, nor as a tonic for
our own minds, but as a means of growing rich, or
of outshining our neighbours in conversation. A
'Dictionary of Thoughts' might, for example, be
useful as a book of reference, and make pleasant
reading for a few idle moments, like Johnson's
Dictionary, or Bartlett's 'Familiar Quotations.'
But it is not for such legitimate usage that we are
counselled to buy it. The volume aspires to have
a social significance, to be a cure-all for the reti-
cence which men value, and for the modesty which
men love. Properly studied, it will enable us to in-
form a shrinking dinner party what Erasmus
thought about humanism, and how Da Vinci felt
about art. Should another guest break into the
conversation with a remark about the disturbed
state of India, or the menace of the Red army, we
can hurl back at him Napoleon's axiom: 'There
are two levers for moving men — interest and

fear'; thus re-focussing attention upon ourselves, and making sure that we will never again be asked to that once friendly board.

Reformatory measures are hailed as cure-alls by people who have a happy confidence in the perfectibility of human nature, and no discouraging acquaintance with history to dim it. The Eighteenth and the Nineteenth Amendments of our Constitution were such gigantic steps, reaching so far and involving so much, that ten or twenty years are periods too short to permit of our forming any reasonable opinion of their value. Indeed, Mr. Brownell has pointed out that the data of human life are unfitted to serve the purpose of theoretic demonstration. It takes more than one generation to test the soundness of men's intelligence, the prophetic vision of their enthusiasms. Senator Borah emphasized this point when he told the Philadelphia Forum that Prohibition had failed in the past because it lacked the sympathy of the nation; but that it would triumph in the future because the sympathy of the nation would be with it.

At present it comes under the head of statutes which Mrs. Gerould has described as passed in the interests of morality, and evaded in the interests of human nature. If it were possible to make a moral law out of a civil law, if it were possible to legislate evil into an innocent thing, or innocence into an evil thing, the path of the legislator would be smooth. A sumptuary law, to be successful, must be in accord with the temperament of the people. Geneva seems to have liked Calvin's rulings. At least it professed to like them; and the worldlings who found them past bearing fled to more habitable towns.

The Eighteenth Amendment deprived the United States of an enormous revenue. Its enforcement costs the taxpayers anywhere from $20,000,000 to $30,000,000 a year. This is a point worthy of consideration. We ought to get something handsome for that money; we ought to be sure that it is something we want, and very sure that none of the millions are misappropriated. So much has been written on the subject that the public has ceased to read any of it. A glance at *Poole's Index* from 1919 to 1931 will show that this was the only life-saving course to pursue. Even the phraseology of the writers no longer calls for comment. The anti-Prohibitionist's urbane allusions to wine and beer, the Prohibitionist's invariable use of the terms 'rum' and 'booze,' illustrate to perfection Mr. Henry Sedgwick's analysis of the prejudices and partisanships of words.

'An indoctrinated and collective virtue,' says Santayana, 'turns easily to fanaticism. It imposes irrational sacrifices.' This is the story of all inquisitions, religious, moral, and political. Torque-

mada never dies. He merely turns his attention
from heresy to some reprobated form of self-gov-
ernment or self-indulgence. And always his inten-
tions are of the best. Always he offers a sharp
remedy for errors to which he is disinclined. Tol-
erance is no less displeasing to him than temper-
ance, which is the child of freedom, the eternal
principle of moderation, inherited by Christianity
from the noblest forms of paganism, and raised to
the glory of a cardinal virtue for the upholding of
the dignity of man.

If the Eighteenth Amendment was admittedly
a measure of reform, a stupendous cure-all designed for the deliverance of the nation, the Nineteenth Amendment would never have been
thought of in these terms, had it not been for the
over-ardent and over-sanguine assertions of its
supporters. It was a measure of reason, of justice,
of legitimate and inevitable progress. Those who
had it at heart saw it — very naturally —
through an illuminated haze, and talked about it
as the promise of a golden age. Enthusiastic fem-
inists, the ones who did the talking, said, and perhaps believed, that women voters would be more
honest and intelligent than men voters, and that
women officials would be more honest and able
than men officials. They assigned to themselves
the glory of 'race-building,' quite as though they
built alone. When they were idealistic, they fore-

told that the religion of women, which is the religion of birth, would replace the religion of men, which is the religion of death. When they were practical, they engaged to clean up politics, clean up streets, and eradicate vice. The city, the state, and the nation are but expansions of the family, and they were prepared to adopt and mother them all.

Now this is not much more than political parties promise at election time. The essence of electioneering is the repeated assertion that the safety of the country and the welfare of its citizens depend on our voting the Republican or the Democratic ticket. Nobody expects the millennium as the result of such voting, but nobody hesitates to predict it. The enfranchisement of women was hailed as a 'world-changing phenomenon.' 'Elevate' was the word most often used to express the working of the new freedom, the new influence in public life. Opponents of the measure accepted their defeat with the good grace of those who were at heart indifferent; and the only people to be pitied were the insistent agitators, who, deprived over-night of a perfectly good cause to agitate, were compelled to fall back on a mad medley of reforms, social, international, psychological, pathological — all of which they urge with an appalling familiarity upon our reluctant consideration.

To expect elevation from the rank and file of

women voters is manifestly absurd. It is also manifestly unjust. If, being less well informed and less experienced than men, they are not less conscientious than men, they give sufficient proof of their fitness to cast a ballot. At present there appears to be some trouble in persuading them to cast it. After listening for years to impassioned appeals for the suffrage, I have listened for subsequent years to impassioned reproaches for its neglect. Clubs and societies have exhorted women to vote. Badges to be worn by those who fulfil this duty have been distributed, and the badgeless ones have been asked to consider themselves as the moral lepers of the community. An active and intelligent minority, which once wrestled for its rights and won them, now faces an apathetic majority, and seeks to compel it to accept its advantages.

A great and growing moderation is noticeable in the public utterances of women. Now and then they get a word of bad advice, as when Lady Astor told them that they could hold the balance of power — which is, let us hope, as impossible as it is undesirable. Holding the balance of power means selling out to the highest bidder, a very demoralizing process. Now and then a genuine sentimentalist like Kathleen Norris, who has failed to outgrow her enthusiasms, finds herself able to speak of women as the crusaders of the body politic. Now and then a hardy fighter like Elizabeth Robins (Parks, not Pennell) asserts with undiminished vigour that the moral power of women is the appointed antidote to the perverted physical power which has hitherto ruled the world. Now and then, but very seldom, a feminist born out of date runs amuck through church and state. A few years ago a writer in the *Century* lifted up her voice in a spirited tirade against Saint Paul, whose very moderate estimate of women — 'sex-embitterment' she called it — stood responsible in her eyes for the failures of Christianity. The 'stuffy asceticism' of the Middle Ages, the 'polluted atmosphere' of the Reformation, the 'follies and brutalities' of our own time — all could be traced back to the Apostle of the Gentiles, and all originated in his imperious masculinity, which the wives and widows of the infant Church were not courageous enough to deny.

An exasperated American politician has said that women's political views defy classification. This is only partially true, and, when it is true, the reason is not far to seek. Party politics are subordinated in the minds of some women to feminism; the desire to advance their own sex, or the deep-rooted conviction that they can serve the world more nobly and more efficiently than it has ever been served by politicians. This is a note which

has been struck more than once by female pacifists, who, of all reformers, can afford to be the
most vehement and the most vague. 'In the matter of war,' wrote Mrs. Carrie Chapman Catt a
few years ago in the *Woman's Home Companion*,
'the women's point of view has asserted itself in
clear contradistinction to men's. It is not only
that women will oppose an individual war when it
comes, but that they will oppose the blunders of
government which cause war.... Women realize
that it is better to lead a nation away from trouble
than to lead it through trouble when trouble
comes.'

It is just possible that men, wise men, have realized this for a few thousand years, and have found
the leading of nations more difficult than the leading of sheep. We have Mr. Root's word for it —
and he ought to know — that 'democracies are
always in trouble.' Yet they are 'cure-alls' themselves, and very high up in the order of deliverance. They may be considered the avenues of approach to the stupendous 'World Republic' which
Mr. Wells holds in reserve as the promised, per-
fected, and permanent panacea for the manifold
ills of humanity.

For this we must look ahead, more patient of
delays than is Mr. Wells, because less sanguine of
results, and bearing in mind the convincing words
of Mr. Irving Babbitt, who says that the wisdom

of the ages (as contrasted with the widsom of the age) has been neither sentimental nor utilitarian, but always religious or humanistic. Always it has had for its inspiration the axiom which France borrowed from older civilizations: 'It is not easy to find happiness in ourselves, and it is not possible to find it elsewhere.' The wisdom of the age (our age) is less deep-rooted, but far more methodical and optimistic. American panaceists, we are told, may be divided into two classes, professionals with whom it is a business and a profitable one, and amateurs with whom it is a religion; who believe that they have remedies for the evils which afflict our own refractory little planet, and who stand ready, like Mr. Gladstone, to reform the solar system. Unshaken enthusiasts, they possess every Christian virtue save humility, without which, said Edmund Burke, the other virtues have no foundation and are of no avail.

Perhaps a profound distaste for the methods of Hapsburgs and Hohenzollerns may have disposed us to concede to democracy a species of holiness, a curative value, not easily analyzed or proved.

> God said, 'I am tired of kings,
> I suffer them no more,'

wrote Emerson in 1863, ascribing his own sentiments to the Almighty, after the time-honoured fashion of men. In 1914, autocracy gave to the world an object lesson in organized and efficient evil that made democracy's blundering incompetence seem like the shining of angels' wings. What if the power of the people is apt to degrade public service to a common level of incapacity! What if intellectual inequalities are as distasteful to it as social inequalities! What if waste, corruption, and folly can be laid to its charge! These sins are not the sins of Cain. They do not cry to Heaven for vengeance; but plead for time, and patience, and renewed confidence in a public conscience, which, though not always an intelligent conscience, is acutely sensitive to direction.

An ingenious theory advanced by Santayana maintains that leadership is immaterial in a pure democracy because of the 'contagious sympathy' of the pure democrats. As soon as the pressure of circumstance necessitates leadership, the pure democracy becomes a rudimentary monarchy. This is true, inasmuch as every government holds in it the rudiments of another form of government. How far the democracy of the United States is a pure democracy, it would be hard to tell. There are those who hold with our kind English critic, Lord Bryce, that we are wholly and triumphantly democratic; and there are those who hold with our caustic Canadian critic, Sir Andrew Macphail, that we are not democratic at all; that in no other civilized country save Russia are the liberties of the people more frequently and systematically raided. One thing is sure. Leadership affects us less than does the contagious sympathy of our fellows. It was not leadership which took us into the Great War — our leaders were men of many minds — it was the contagious sympathy of pure democrats who, like Emerson, were tired of the ways of kings.

Plato, whose words have a curious fashion of sounding as if they had been spoken the day before yesterday, says that democracy is 'a charming form of government, full of variety and disorder, which dispenses equality alike to equals and unequals.' Even little lapdogs, he observes, walk about consequentially, with their noses in the air, and get out of nobody's way. Criminals are treated benevolently. Men condemned to exile or to death are neither exiled nor executed. They 'just stay where they are,' and, when they appear in public, affect the demeanour of heroes.

Translated into slang, this paragraph might appear any day in any newspaper as the observation of a ribald American humourist. It will be remembered that Lord Bryce admitted that we were an 'indulgent' people, and that our courts of justice could thole amends. It was also plain to his regard that democracy as an institution fails to vivify intellectual life. But he most firmly believed that, for all its difficulties in a country subject to unresting immigration, it makes for methodical progress, and that it embodies a spirit of hopefulness, not to be found elsewhere. This last asset is our heaviest and our best. 'The mapped lands and chartered waters of orderly development' lie well within our reach. If misdirected effort sidetracks us, we are not the only travellers through life who must retrace our steps. And if the worst comes to worst, and the measure of accomplishment is always unfulfilled, then surely everlasting hope is no bad cure-all for the sadness of an imperfect world.

'For every age,' said the melancholy Conrad, 'is fed on illusions, lest men should renounce life early, and the human race come to an end.'

What is Moral Support?

IN THE 'News of the Day,' as presented five
years ago in a moving-picture hall, there was
shown to the audience a photograph of President Coolidge speaking in Cambridge, Massachusetts, on the one hundred and fiftieth anniversary
of Washington's taking command of the Colonial
forces. The caption read: 'President holds out
helping hand to Europe.'

Naturally the photographer did not know what
was in Mr. Coolidge's outstretched hand; but the
reporters for the press were better informed. The
headlines of one newspaper ran thus: 'Coolidge
Bids Europe Frame Security Pacts. Pledges
Moral Support of United States, But Specifically
Excepts Political Participation.' An editorial in
another newspaper of the same date emphasized
the President's approval of 'mutual covenants for
mutual security,' and quoted to this effect from
his speech: 'While our country should refrain
from making political commitments where it does
not have political interests, such covenants would
always have the moral support of our Government.'

Words have a meaning. It is all that gives them
value. Therefore the two words 'moral support'

must have a tangible significance in the minds of those who use them. Henry Adams, who hated mental confusion, and had the prevailing discontent of the clear-sighted, said that morality was a private and costly luxury. 'Masses of men invariably follow interests in deciding morals.' Yet, while Americans are frankly and reasonably determined to let their own interests dictate their policies, they retain morality as a political weapon, or at least as a political slogan. They offer the approbation of the American conscience as something which is directly or indirectly an asset to the nations of Europe. If they are acute, as was President Coolidge, they admit that the financing of foreign enterprise is a matter of policy. If they are blatant, as is the occasional habit of politicians, they intimate that moral support is a species of largesse in the gift of moral leadership, and that moral leadership is a recognized attribute of size and numbers, as exemplified by the United States. Like the little girl who was so good that she knew how good she was, we are too well-informed not to be aware of our preëminence in this field.

In the spring of 1925 the American Ambassador at the Court of Saint James's delivered himself of a speech before the Pilgrims' Dinner in London. In it he defined with great precision the attitude of the United States toward her former allies. His remarks, as reported, read like a sermon preached in a reformatory; but it is possible that they had a more gracious sound when delivered urbanely over the wine glasses, and that the emphasis laid upon 'the position of the plain people of America toward the reconstruction of Europe' was less contemptuous than it appeared in print.

'The full measure of American helpfulness,' said our representative, 'can be obtained only when the American people are assured that the time for destructive methods and policies has passed, and that the time for peaceful upbuilding has come. They are asking themselves today if that time has, in fact, arrived, and they cannot answer the question. The reply must come from the people of Europe, who alone can make the decision. If it be peace, then you may be sure that America will help to her generous utmost. But if the issue shall continue to be confused and doubtful, I fear the helpful processes which are now in motion must inevitably cease. We are not, as a people, interested in making speculative advances. We can undertake to help only those who help themselves.'

I try to imagine these words addressed to an American audience by a British official (presuming conditions were reversed), and I hear the deep-mouthed profanity rising from the heart to the lips of every American who listened to them. If we were taxing ourselves to the utmost in order to repay a debt to Great Britain, profanity would seem to be in order. Yet the American press in general expressed no distaste for such lofty hectoring. Editors reminded us that it 'did no more than state the feeling of the nation'; that it sounded a 'timely warning' to Europeans who counted on our aid; and that it was 'in the nature of an ultimatum from one hundred and ten millions of Americans.'

Our passion for counting heads is occasionally misleading. If one hundred and ten millions of Americans acquiesced seemingly in this 'timely warning' to our creditors, it was because one hundred million knew little, and cared less, about the matter. The comments of the foreign press were naturally of an ironic order, though the London *Times* took the wind out of our sails by acquiescing cordially in our Ambassador's views, and congratulating the United States on its 'coöperation with Great Britain in the task of reconstructing Europe'; thus robbing us of the lead with a graceful and friendly gesture, and a reminder that England had yet to be paid the debts her allies owed her. The Paris *Temps*, on the other hand, offered with exaggerated courtesy the suggestion that France was endeavouring to follow America's advice to help herself, and was at that very moment engaged in repairing the devastations wrought by an invading army purposed to de-

stroy. She was 'peacefully upbuilding' her shattered towns. As for the Berlin newspapers, they
seemed unanimously disposed to consider both
the speech and the ensuing discussion as personal
affronts to von Hindenburg.

The interesting criticisms from my point of
view were contributed by the *Cleveland Press*, the
New York Evening Post, and the *New York Times*.
The *Cleveland Press* generously regretted that 'our
highly desired and much sought moral helpfulness
had been conspicuously withheld from Europe.'
The *Post* said with severity: 'The aid we are now
giving, whether monetary or moral, will come to
an end unless good faith and mutual trust drive
out hatred and mistrust.' The *Times*, with the
habitual restraint of a vastly influential newspaper, contented itself with observing that 'the
Administration seems to believe the time has
come for a show-down, and that Europe must display more earnestness in settling her own affairs
if she is to keep on asking for America's moral and
monetary support.'

Here were three clear-cut recognitions of moral,
as apart from financial or political support, and
three clear-cut intimations that moral support is
in itself a thing of value which the nations of
Europe would be loath to lose. Yet I cannot think
that any one of those three journals seriously considered that England and France covet our esteem

any more than they covet the esteem of the rest of
the world. Why should they? Every nation must
respect itself, and make that self-respect the goal
and guerdon of all effort. 'Great tranquillity of
heart hath he who careth neither for praise nor
blame,' wrote à Kempis; and the single-mindedness of the man who has some better purpose than
to please is but a reflex of the single-mindedness of
the nation which reveres its own traditions and
ideals too deeply to make them interchangeable
with the traditions and ideals of other nations.

Suppose Italy were to threaten the United
States with the withdrawal of her moral support.
How droll the idea would be! Yet Italy is a country civilized to the core. Her ignorance is often
less crude than is information elsewhere; her
methods of approach have in them the charm of
immemorial amenities. She is as seriously religious as we are; and her people are more law-abid-
ing than ours, perhaps because they are given less
choice in the matter. There is every reason why
Rome and Washington should respect each other,
and be as morally helpful to each other as they
know how to be; but there is no reason on earth
why the moral support of one should be of more
value than the moral support of the other, unless
we translate morality into terms of strength and
wealth.

This is what the Governor of Wisconsin did

when he besought President Coolidge to make no
terms for the settlement of the French debts until
the war in Morocco was ended. He assumed our
moral right to dictate the foreign policies of France
because France owed us money; and he assumed
that America was qualified to decide what was
right and what was wrong in Morocco because she
was the creditor nation. He earnestly desired that
our Government, by refusing negotiations with
France, should lend its moral support to the Riffs,
who are formidable fighters, and who would have
been amazed rather than flattered if they had
known how they were being written about in sympathetic American newspapers. 'The murder of
helpless, defenseless women and children,' was
a picturesque, rather than an exact, description
of the campaigns of Marshals Lyautey and Pétain
in Morocco.

As there is nothing new under the sun, history
supplies us with more than one instance of moral
support offered in place of material assistance,
and always by a nation strong enough to give
weight to such an unsubstantial commodity. The
great Elizabeth dealt largely in it because it cost
her nothing, won the approval of her subjects, indicated her authority, nourished her sense of om-
niscience, and gave opportunity for the noble
wording (she was a past mistress of words) of purposes never destined to be fulfilled.

How superbly, yet how economically, the
Queen placed England on record as the champion
of the oppressed, when, after the Massacre of
Saint Bartholomew, she draped herself and her
court in mourning before consenting to receive the
importunate French Ambassador! What a magnificent gesture of grief and stern repudiation! It
is probable that the unlucky Frenchman felt himself as embarrassed as he was meant to be, though
he knew perfectly well that Elizabeth had never
kept her 'fair promises' to Coligny, and that she
had no mind to discontinue her international
flirtation with the Duke d'Alençon, merely because his royal mother stood responsible for the
murder of a few thousand French Protestants.
He accepted the rebuff to his country as disagree-
able but not dangerous, and created a diversion
by producing a letter from d'Alençon — one of the
many amorous epistles which passed between
these make-believe lovers — which was very gra-
ciously received. Notwithstanding the fact that
England was filled with 'an extreme indignation
and a marvellous hatred,' the Ambassador was
able, six weeks after his humiliating reception, to
write to Catherine that the English Queen would
stand firmly by her alliance with France.

The relations between Elizabeth and Catherine
de' Medici form an engaging page of history.
Their correspondence is to be recommended as a

complete course in duplicity. Both were accomplished liars, and each politely professed to believe the other's lies. Catherine cherished the preposterous hope that the English Queen would marry one of her sons. Elizabeth had no such intention; but she liked — Heaven knows why! — to pretend that she would. Her only bond with Catherine was their mutual fear and hatred of Spain. It was a heavy cross to her that she could not weaken France without strengthening Spain. Providence was hard on her in this matter. Providence was hard on her in the matter of the rebellious Netherlands, and in the matter of John Knox. She never wanted to give more than moral support to any cause, and she was constantly being pushed to the fore by virtue of the power she held.

The Protestant insurgents in the Netherlands had the sympathy of England. William of Nassau was a hero in English eyes, and Burghley stoutly advocated his cause. The London merchants, always practical, raised a force at their own expense, and shipped it to Rotterdam, with Sir Humphrey Gilbert at its head. But Elizabeth held back her hand. It was not only that she hated to spend the money, and not only that she was by nature incapable of committing herself generously to any principle. It was that in her heart of hearts this daughter of the Tudors disapproved of subjects opposing their sovereigns. She was a sovereign herself, and she knew that fomenting rebellion is like throwing a boomerang. Being at odds with the Pope, she would lend moral support to the French Protestants; and, being at odds with Spain, she would lend moral support to the Dutch insurgents. This was in accord with her own conscience and with the conscience of England. But, like conscientious America a few centuries later, she would 'refrain from making political commitments where she did not have political interests.'

With the same caution, and the same characteristic understanding of her own position, Elizabeth was content that John Knox should harass the Queen Regent, Mary of Guise, and, later on, the young Queen of Scots. Such harassments were commendable, as being a species of warfare against the Church of Rome. But as for permitting this firebrand, this arrogant defamer of feminine sovereignty, to set foot on English soil, she would as soon have thought of raising John Stubbs to the peerage. Her cold and vigorous understanding set at naught the protestations of a man who had presumed unwisely on her indulgence. So did the great Tsaritsa, Catherine, regard the Lutheran and Calvinistic clergymen to whom she had lent her moral support when they were conveniently remote; and who, confiding in her goodwill, actually sought to enter Holy Russia, and build their chapels at her doors.

The interest felt by France in the rebellious American Colonies was called sympathy, an intelligible word with a modest and a friendly sound. The cause of the Colonists was extolled as the sacred cause of liberty. Franklin, like Mrs. Jarley, was 'the delight of the nobility and gentry.' If the French Government delayed sending money and men until the American arms showed some reasonable chance of success, it stood ready to turn that chance into a certainty. Louis the Sixteenth cherished a sentimental regard for principles which eventually conducted him to the scaffold. He gave Franklin six million francs out of his own deplenished purse; and the citizens of Franklin's town repaid him by hailing with indecent glee the news of his execution. It is to be noted that the logical French mind never disregarded America's real needs. France took no great risks; but neither did she offer her esteem as an actual asset to the Colonies.

So 'moral support' still defies analysis. The phrase appears and reappears without gaining significance. Count Karolyi, President of the short-lived 'People's Republic' of Hungary, a man of many grievances, and of many words with which to voice them, declared angrily that he was not permitted to appeal to Americans because his unworthy country feared the withdrawal of America's 'moral and financial support.' A paradoxical writer in the *World's Work* has intimated that the United States, being congested with money, stands in especial need of Europe's 'moral support' — a novel, but not a clarifying point of view. The only nation that makes its meaning plain is Russia. Her moral support is always translatable into solid substantialities. Moscow makes no boast of wealth; her people, indeed, give unenviable indications of poverty; but she can afford a strong standing army, and she can afford foreign propaganda on a scale of well-considered lavishness. While America puts on weight and wisdom, Russia puts on speed and dynamic force. America will mend the world in her way, Russia will mend it in hers; and the beautiful, dangerous world, which cannot be 'dry-docked for repairs,' is patched here and there with amazing ingenuity as it spins on its unresting way.

On a Certain Condescension in Americans

SIXTY–TWO years ago Mr. James Russell Lowell published in the *Atlantic Monthly* an urbanely caustic essay, 'On a Certain Condescension in Foreigners.' Despite discursiveness (it was a leisurely age), this *Apologia pro patria sua* is a model of good temper, good taste, and good feeling. Its author regretted England's dislike for our accent, France's distaste for our food, and Germany's contempt for our music; but he did not suffer himself to be cast down. With a modesty past all praise, he even admitted, what no good American will admit today, that popular government 'is no better than any other form except as the virtue and wisdom of the people make it so'; and that self-made men 'may not be divinely commissioned to fabricate the higher qualities of opinion on all possible topics of human interest.' Nevertheless, he found both purpose and principle in the young nation, hammered into shape by four years of civil war. 'One might be worse off than even in America,' mused this son of Massachusetts; and we are instantly reminded of William James's softly breathed assurance: 'A Yankee is also, in the last analysis, one of God's creatures.'

Sixty-two years are but a small fragment of time. Not long enough surely for the civilization of Europe to decay, and the civilization of the United States to reach a pinnacle of splendour. Yet the condescension which Mr. Lowell deprecated, and which was based upon superiority of culture, seems like respectful flattery compared to the condescension which Americans now daily display, and which is based upon superiority of wealth. There has been no startling decline of European institutions, no magnificent upbuilding of our own; only a flow of gold from the treasuries of London, Paris, and Rome into the treasury of Washington. Germany's belief in the economic value of war, fruit of the evil seed sown in 1870, has been realized in a fashion which Germans least expected. England is impoverished in money and men. The casualties in the British army were over three million; the killed numbered six hundred and fifty-eight thousand. France is impoverished in money, men, and resources. A conscientious destruction of everything that might prove profitable if spared marked the progress of the invading Teutons. But the tide of wealth did not flow to Berlin. It leaped the sea, and filled the coffers of the nation that had provided the sinews of war, and that had turned the tide of victory.

Under these circumstances the deep exhaustion

of countries that have been struggling for life
as a drowning man struggles for breath, is hardly
a matter for surprise. Cause and effect are too
closely linked to need elucidation. That such
countries should have recovered some measure of
order, of reason, of normal energy, and of a
Heaven-sent capacity for enjoyment, is the
blessed miracle of our century. The superb
conservation of force, which Mr. Galsworthy
says makes it difficult to come to the end of an
Englishman, has held him uncrushed under a
load of taxation which would have broken
the heart and hopes of any other people. The
strength and invulnerability of France's creative
instinct, her unfailing respect for individual distinction, have filled her national life with something besides care. Our admiration for such
qualities in no wise lessens our liking for our own
civilization, our preference for what is ours and
for what suits us best; but it might save us from a
blinding and naïvely spoken self-esteem.

A year or two ago Governor A. Harry Moore of
New Jersey made an address to the congregation
of the First Presbyterian Church of Manasquan.
It was a patriotic address, and, as such, followed
the formula which invariably refers our goodness
and greatness to the active partnership of God.
'The world,' said Governor Moore, 'is waiting
for America. It leaps to hear every blow America

strikes. America shines among nations as the little child that shall lead them. Just as God gave humanity a new chance when He directed Noah to build the Ark, so He gave it a new chance when He put it into the head of an Italian navigator to discover America.'

My excuse for quoting these words is that they were spoken by an official, printed by a representative newspaper, and read by the general public. They may therefore be considered as representing one layer of the American adult mind. The suggestion of an ex-governor of Iowa that we should expel from our country all foreigners who cannot recite the Constitution of the United States and Lincoln's 'Gettysburg Address,' represents a second layer. The ultimatum of a popular evangelist: 'If I had my way there would be no language but English taught in the United States, and any immigrant coming here and not speaking our tongue would be immediately sent back,' represents a third. Or perhaps they are one and the same. Now it is all very well for an ironical scientist, like Dr. Joseph Collins, to intimate that there is no such thing as an American adult mind, and that the great body of the people think like children until they reach senility, and cease thinking at all. The fact remains that nobody but a moron has any right to think like a child after he has ceased to be one.

He may go on doing it because it is an easy, pleasant, and self-sufficient thing for him to do. But the value of our thinking is the test of our civilization. If we apprehend the exact nature of our offering to the great depositories of human thought, we know where we stand in the orderly progress of the ages.

There does not seem to be much doubt on this score in the mind (I must continue to use the word) of the average American. The *Atlantic Monthly* published in February, 1924, a paper by Mr. Langdon Mitchell on 'The American Malady.' The writer quoted a few lines from an editorial in the *Ladies' Home Journal*, August, 1923: 'There is only one first-class civilization in the world today. It is right here in the United States and the Dominion of Canada. Europe's is hardly second-class, and Asia's is about fourth- to sixth-class.' I verified this quotation, finding it a little difficult to credit, and borrowed it for a lecture I was giving in New York. My audience took it at its face value, and cheerfully, I might say enthusiastically, applauded the sentiment. It was evident that to them it was a modest statement of an incontrovertible fact, and they registered their cordial agreement. They seemed — so far as I could apprehend them — to believe that we were, like the Jews, a chosen people, that our mission was the 'uplift' of the human race, and that it behooved those who were to be uplifted to recognize their inferior altitude.

Is this an unusual frame of mind among educated Americans? Is it confined to Main Street, or to the film actress who told Paris reporters that the United States was forty years (why forty?) ahead of Europe 'intellectually and morally'? Where can we find a better spokesman for the race than Mr. Walter Hines Page, a man to whom was given a hard and heartrending job, who did it superlatively well (even the animadversions of his critics are based upon the success of his activities), and who died in the doing of it, worn out, body and soul and mind, as if he had been shot to pieces in the trenches? Yet this able and representative American thought and said that Latin civilization was a negligible asset to the world. He could see little good in people who did not speak English, and no good at all in people who did not speak English or French. 'Except the British and the French,' he wrote to his son, Arthur Page, in December, 1917, 'there's no nation in Europe worth a tinker's damn when you come to the real scratch. The whole continent is rotten, or tyrannical, or yellow dog. I wouldn't give Long Island or Moore County for the whole of continental Europe.'

It was a curious estimate of values. Long Island is a charming place, and very rich. Moore

County is, I doubt not, one of the most beautiful tracts in a supremely beautiful State. Nevertheless, there are those who would think them dearly bought at the price of Rome. No one can truly say that Switzerland, Denmark, and Holland are rotten, or tyrannical, or yellow dog. Indeed, Mr. Page admitted that the Danes were a free people, and that Switzerland was a true republic, but too small to count — a typically American point of view. To interpret life in terms of size and numbers rather than in terms of intellect, beauty, and goodness is natural for a patriot who has more than three million square miles of country, and over a hundred million countrymen. As Walt Whitman lustily sang:

> I dote on myself — there is that lot of me, and all so luscious.

That Mr. Page clearly foresaw the wealth and strength that would accrue to the United States from the World War proves the keenness of his vision. In 1914 he wrote to President Wilson: 'From an economic point of view, we *are* the world; and from a political point of view also.' That he was sure this wealth and strength were well placed proves the staunchness of his civic pride. 'In all the humanities, we are a thousand years ahead of any people here,' was his summing-up in a letter to Mr. Frank Doubleday, 1916. Even

our reluctance to credit Prussia with militarism
showed the immaculate innocence of our hearts.
'There could be no better measure of the moral
advance that the United States has made over
Europe than the incredulity of our people.'
Finally, in a burst of enthusiasm, or sentiment,
or perhaps homesickness, comes a magnificent
affirmation and elucidation of our august pre-
eminence: 'God has as yet made nothing or nobody equal to the American people; and I don't
think He ever will or can.' Which is a trifle fetter-
ing to omnipotence.

Mr. Page's Americanism being what it was,
I cannot help thinking that his countrymen
might have more readily forgiven his admiration
for the admittedly inferior qualities of Great
Britain. His regard for England was not wholly
unlike the regard of the English for the United
States in Mr. Lowell's day: a friendly feeling,
made friendlier by a definite and delightful consciousness of superiority. Ten months before the
war, he wrote to President Wilson: 'The future of
the world belongs to us.... Now what are we
going to do with this leadership when it falls
into our hands? And how can we use the English
for the highest purposes of democracy?'

The last sentence is a faultless expression of
national condescension. It would have given
Mr. Lowell as much entertainment as did the

comments of his British acquaintances. I know
nothing to put by its side, because it is so kindly
meant. Our lordliness is, as a rule, a trifle more
severe, tinged with reproof rather than sweetened
with patronage. When the Locarno Conference
progressed to its satisfactory conclusion without
our help or hindrance, a leading American newspaper seized the opportunity (which was not a
good opportunity) to assert our domination over
Europe, and to remind her of the finality of our
verdicts. If our President urged 'international
agreements,' his words must be received outside
the United States as 'a warning that this government, as represented by Mr. Coolidge, will accept
no excuse for war anywhere.'

But why, in heaven's name, should any
European nation have offered an excuse to Mr.
Coolidge for anything it felt disposed to do?
If it belonged to the League of Nations, and
undertook, however lamely, to go to war on its
own account, excuses were in order, but not to
Washington. Even in the World Court we share
our rights and responsibilities with other Governments, and accept or reject excuses in accordance
with the will of the majority.

The Locarno Treaty does, in fact, give us food
for thought. It in no way impairs our safety or
our interests. We are as big and as strong and as
rich as we were before. But it shows us that

something can be accomplished without our controlling influence. Our help is needed in the reconstruction of battered Europe; but, while we can withhold it at pleasure, giving it does not warrant too sharp a tone of authority. A little boy, who has since grown into a distinguished man of letters, once stepped with deliberation into a pond, and stood there to the detriment of his health and of his shoes. An indignant aunt summoned him to dry land. The little boy, being well out of reach, remained waterlogged and defiant. The aunt, indisposed to pursuit, said sternly: 'Do you know what I do when youngsters refuse to obey me! I whip them.' The little boy, aware of moral as well as of physical immunity, replied with decision: 'You don't vip other people's children, I pwesume.' And neither, when it comes to the point, does the United States.

It is natural, though regrettable that inferior nations, crowded together in Europe which they have somehow contrived to make glorious and beautiful ('Thank God,' cried Henry James, 'for a world which holds so rich an England, so rare an Italy!'), should resent our presenting ourselves to them as an example. They have troubles and traditions of their own, inheritances great and grievous which reach back to

> ... old, unhappy, far-off things,
> And battles long ago.

They cannot wipe the slate clean, and begin afresh after a new and improved model. We keep on telling them (I quote now from recent American utterances) that our 'accumulated heritage of spiritual blessings' is theirs to command; that our idealism 'has made itself felt as a great contributory force in the advancement of mankind,' and that 'the Stars and Stripes are a harbinger of a new and happier day for the lesser nations of the world.' We explain to them that if we have demanded payment of their debts it was in order to maintain 'the principle of the integrity of international obligations'; and that our connection with a World Court is in the nature of a public notice 'that the enormous influences of our country are to be cast on the side of the enlightened processes of civilization.' 'Lord, gie us a guid conceit o' ourselves,' is about the only prayer which the American has no need to utter.

If Europeans pay insufficient regard to our carefully catalogued virtues, Americans are far too deeply impressed by them. It is as demoralizing for a nation to feel itself an ethical exhibit as it is demoralizing for a young woman to win a beauty prize in an Atlantic City contest. The insult offered to our country by calling such a prize-winner 'Miss America' is not greater than the insult offered to our country by calling every expansive wave of self-esteem 'Americanism.'

If our civilization be 'infinitely the best so far developed in the ages,' we have all the less need to say so. If we are giving to the world 'supreme grandeur in service,' we can afford to be modest in calling attention to the fact. If we are, by virtue of precept and example, 'working great changes in the spirit of international morality,' it would be more self-respecting to give other nations a chance to express their unprodded appreciation and gratitude.

America has invested her religion as well as her morality in sound income-paying securities. She has adopted the unassailable position of a nation blessed because it deserves to be blessed; and her sons, whatever other theologies they may affect or disregard, subscribe unreservedly to this national creed. Scholars, men of letters, and the clergy lend it their seasonable support. Professor Thomas Nixon Carver of Harvard, who has written a clear, forceful, and eminently readable book on 'The Present Economic Revolution in the United States,' seems to have no shadow of doubt that our good fortune, which might be better, is due to our good behaviour, which cannot be improved on. 'Prosperity is coming to us,' he says, 'precisely because our ideals are not materialistic. It is coming to us because we are pursuing the exalted ideal of equality under liberty, as it must of necessity come to any nation that pursues that ideal whole-heartedly and enthusiastically.... All these things are being added to us precisely because we are seeking the Kingdom of God and His righteousness, as they are always added, and must of logical necessity always be added, unto any nation that seeks those ideals of justice which are the very essence of the Kingdom of God.'

I wonder if righteousness can be linked so securely to the elements of success; and if food and raiment — all that is promised in the Gospel — can be magnified into the colossal fortunes of America. The American may not be materialistic; but he has certainly hallowed commercialism, and made of it both a romantic and a moral adventure. He sings its saga at banquets, and he relates its conquests to his sons in magazines and in much-read books. There is great satisfaction in doing this, and we are told it is well done. If something be lacking in such a philosophy, that something is not missed. It is easy to count up the value of the proprieties in a watchful world; but exceedingly hard to put the spiritual life on a paying basis. The Old Testament consistently taught that goodness and piety were rewarded with material well-being; but Christianity has committed itself to no such untenable proposition. 'He that findeth his life shall lose it,' sounds inconceivably remote from the contemplation of well-merited affluence.

A point of difference between the condescension of foreigners in 1869 and the condescension of Americans in 1931 is that the magniloquence which amused and ruffled Mr. Lowell was mainly spoken (he was in a position to hear it both at home and abroad), and the magniloquence which today ruffles, without amusing, sensitive foreigners and Americans is, as I have shown by liberal quotations, printed for all the reading world to see. An editorial in *Current Opinion* modestly suggests that 'Europeans might learn a good deal if they would come over here, study the history of America since the war, and try to imitate our example .... We may be crass and uncultured; but at least we have been good sports, and have been honest enough, farsighted enough, and sagacious enough to render the United States the soundest and healthiest nation in the world today.'

A 'good sport' recognizes handicaps. He knows and he admits that poverty is not the equivalent of wealth, that dead men are not equal to live men, that ruined towns are less habitable than whole ones. A 'good sport' may honestly believe that the one hope for mankind is 'the Americanization of the world'; but he does not coarsely call on Europe to 'clean up and pay up'; he does not write with comprehensive ignorance: 'Europeans will have to abandon their national vanities, and get together, before they can expect to get together

with us'; he does not second the Congressman from
Ohio who informed the American Chamber of
Commerce in London that 'right now the United
States wants to see Europe do some housecleaning
without delay.' He may have even ventured a
doubt when the Honorable David F. Houston,
writing ably and reasonably in *Harper's Magazine*,
June, 1924, affirmed our superior spotlessness.
'The United States,' said Mr. Houston, 'is in a
position of leadership in all the fundamental idealistic, moral, and spiritual forces which make a
nation great, and constitute a worthy civilization.
It seeks as its highest aim to have a clean national
household from cellar to attic.'

Seeks it, yes. All civilized countries seek political integrity, and justice in the administration of
law. Sufficiency, security, and freedom are not the
exclusive ideals of the United States. We may be
as good as we are great, but our distaste for sincere
and searching criticism blurs our national vision.
A blustering, filibustering, narrow-minded Senate
is not a source of legitimate pride. To lead the
world in crime should be a source of legitimate
humiliation. President Coolidge called the attention of the State Governors in January, 1926, to
the fact that twenty-four thousand persons had
met their deaths by highway fatalities within
twelve months. He said it was too many for one
country in one year, and he was right. Yet twenty-

four thousand deaths by accidents — some of which were unavoidable — are less appalling than eleven thousand deaths by violence in the same length of time. The combined numbers are worth the consideration of peace-loving Americans who write eloquently about the sacredness of life.

The crime waves in every State of the Union have now reached a stage of permanent inundation; and the ever-increasing youthfulness of criminals (the American Bar Association has called our attention to this point) promises more complete submergence in the future. It is gratifying to know that twenty-odd million American children go to our schools every day; but some of them appear to spare time from their studies for the more exciting pursuits of robbery, house-breaking, and pathetically premature attempts at banditry; to say nothing of such higher flights as firing their schools, and murdering their grandmothers. These lawless infants are the distinctive product of our age. Their years are few, but their delinquencies are many. If they keep on getting younger and younger, and more and more murderously inclined, we shall after a while be afraid to pass a baby in a perambulator.

The *Ladies' Home Journal* has recently told us that 'everywhere in Europe the ambitious youngsters of the new generation are learning English, and studying American geography and political

history. They want to get the spirit of what
American democracy really is.' We cannot but
hope that these innocent offspring of effete civilizations will not extend their studies to American
newspapers. If they do, they may give their back-
ward countries a rude jolt. In 1926, Scotland,
with a population of five millions, had only eleven
murders, while Massachusetts, with a population
of four millions, could boast of one hundred and
seven. Mr. Francis B. Sayre, writing for the *Atlantic Monthly* in June, 1928, says that more rob-
beries are committed every year in Cleveland
(which used to be an innocent-looking town) than
in England, Scotland, and Wales. Also that for
every ten murders committed in London, one
hundred and sixty are committed in New York;
and that seven out of London's ten murderers are
hanged, while one out of New York's hundred and
sixty are electrocuted. It almost seems as though
we could do a little housecleaning of our own.

The superiority complex is, however, as impervious to fact as to feeling. It denies the practical,
it denies the intellectual, and it denies the spiritual. The Sorbonne and the Institut Pasteur make
no more appeal to it than does the girl, Jeanne
d'Arc, or the defenders of Verdun. France as the
inspiration of the artist, the stimulus of the
thinker, the home of those who seek to breathe
the keen air of human intelligence, is lost in the

France whose stabilized franc is worth four cents of 'real' American money. She is, in our eyes, a nation reprehensible because she demands the security which two oceans guarantee to us, and contemptible because she has failed to readjust herself after such calamities as we have never known.

What the American likes and respects is what he is happy enough to possess: efficiency, moral uniformity, and a fairly good brand of standardized thought. Conventions are the life and soul of the country, and there is nothing like a convention (except perhaps a political campaign) for making us think well of ourselves. The importunate virtues of small communities are nourished by oratory, and by uplift-mongers on platforms, and in the editorial columns of widely circulated periodicals. Uplifting has become a vocation, and its practitioners enjoy the esteem and gratitude of the public. 'Every American,' says André Siegfried, 'is at heart an evangelist.' If he isn't, it is felt that he ought to be. There is a poignantly funny description in one of William James's letters of a lady, the wife of a Methodist minister whom he met at Chautauqua, who told him she had his portrait hanging in her bedroom, and underneath it these words: 'I want to bring balm to human lives.' 'Supposed,' said the horrified — and modest — philosopher, 'to be a quotation from *me!*'

Americanism has been defined as 'the more or

less perfect expression of the common belief that American ideals realize themselves in American society.' This belief is wholly disassociated from the austere creed of the patriot. It was not patriotism which made foreigners in Mr. Lowell's day so sure that they were conferring a favour on the United States by visiting our shores. It is not patriotism which makes Americans today so sure that they are conferring a benefit on Europe by advice and admonition, by bidding her study our methods and imitate our example. There is an intellectual humility which is another name for understanding. It enables us to measure the depths of tragedies which have brought us no personal pain, and the heights of supremacies which have failed to arouse our ambitions. It is the key to history, and the open-sesame to the hearts of men. It may even come as close to deciphering the mysterious ways of God as does the complete assurance that we are His deservedly favourite children.

Santayana says that goodwill is the great American virtue, but that it lacks direction. It should, if it be a veritable virtue, save us outright from the cruel pleasure of contrast, which we are too often bidden to enjoy, and which we confuse in our minds with gratitude for the gifts of Heaven. The sorrowful burden of human knowledge is ours to bear. The dark places of the earth are not confined to other continents than ours. Efficiency is an asset; but without a well balanced emotional life it gets us no further than the door of happiness. Peace and wealth are serviceable possessions; but only intense personalities can create art and letters. It takes a great deal to make an enjoyable world. It takes all we have to give to make a world morally worthy of man.

Actor and Audience

WE KNOW what an audience sees when the curtain rises, and it looks upon the lighted stage; but what do the actors see in their mind's eye when they look upon the darkened house? We know what the audience hears when it listens to the spoken lines; but what do the actors hear in the heavy silence, the restless movements, the misplaced laughter of the crowd? We know what the audience feels when the drama is unfolded, and scene after scene carries us to the appointed climax; but what do the actors feel when the long dim rows of men and women follow, or fail to follow, the movement of the play? A vast literature has been written about the stage from the point of view of the critic who speaks for the audience; but very little has been written about the audience from the point of view of the actor who speaks for himself, and that little is seldom of an enlightening character. Yet the audience is the controlling factor in the actor's life. It is practically infallible, since there is no appeal from its verdict. It is a little like a supreme court composed of irresponsible minors.

No people in the world have been more in-

defatigable than players in writing their rem-
iniscences.   They have filled fat volumes with
anecdotes and adventures which make good
reading, but which fail to clarify the subtle relations between themselves and the public. We
listen to what they have had to say from the days
of Colley Cibber to the days of George Cohan,
and we are vastly entertained; but save for a few
words here and there — noticeably from Mr.
Arliss — we learn little of what we want to
know.   The comments of the discontented have
naturally a keener edge than have the comments
of the complacent who appear to be immune
from misgivings, and who are certainly immune
from the subtle vice of self-depreciation.   To
Mrs. Patrick Campbell, for example, an audience
is but another name for an 'ovation.' Her volume is one long record of 'tremendous applause'
and 'tumultuous enthusiasm.' Whenever I had
the pleasure of seeing this handsome and, on the
whole, satisfactory actress, the house was like
most American houses, good-natured and un-
critical; but there were apparently other nights
in other towns when it 'sat breathless,' or burst
into 'roars of delight,' and when she herself was
'stupefied' by the fervour of its responsiveness.
Compared to such triumphs the successes of her
contemporaries are tame and insipid. It is not
from Mrs. Patrick Campbell that we shall learn

anything of value about that most uncertain of entities, an audience.

Aristotle complained that the Greeks wanted happy endings to their plays. So do Americans. The Greeks seldom got what they desired, being recreated for the most part by dramas which were eminently calculated to lessen the innocent gayety of life. Americans refuse to grant more than a *succès d'estime* to any play which is logically and inexorably sad. In this connection it is interesting to note Ellen Terry's assertion that she played Ophelia (a part for which she was ill-fitted) better in Chicago than in any other American city, because the Chicagoans evinced a downright pity — which she sensed — for the unhappy heroine's plight. Also that John Barrymore found the West to be more in sympathy with Galsworthy's merciless drama, *Justice*, than was the Atlantic coast; and that the sombre beauty of *Peter Ibbetson* made a stronger appeal in Canada than anywhere in the United States. Mr. Barrymore believed that this was because so many young Canadians had perished in the war.

Comments so well considered carry us as far as we are likely to get into the no man's land which lies between the actor and the audience. They are at any rate more helpful than records of ovations and mishaps. Mr. Arliss, a very keen observer, confesses that he found himself con-

fronted by enigmas which he solved with difficulty. He reached the conclusion that the coldness
with which *Disraeli* was first received in the
States was due to the haziness of historical
association in the mind of the average American.
Unless he were a Jew, he knew uncommonly
little about the subject matter of the play; and
it was some time before he felt himself sufficiently
at home and at ease to enjoy a flawless piece of
character acting. In London the trouble lay the
other way around. Englishmen remembered too
much of their own recent history to relish the
liberties taken by the dramatist. The consensus
of opinion seemed to be that if the Bank of England had had such a faltering fool for a president,
Britain never could or would have controlled the
Suez Canal.

Mr. Arliss has real views concerning audiences.
He insists that sometimes — though rarely —
they have a magnetic quality which stimulates
and inspires the actor, and that this quality is
most manifest in their silence, 'vibrating as it
does with sympathetic interest and understanding.' He goes so far as to admit that an actor becomes occasionally interested in his audience,
feels a friendly relationship, and thanks Heaven
it has imagination enough to supplement his
inadequacies, to help him 'out of many a tight
place.' At the same time there is a certain sense

oi hostility, or at least of battle, in his casual comparison of the average audience to an unfriendly animal: 'Let it see you are afraid of it, and it will snap at you; face it boldly, and it will eat out of your hand.'

This sentiment is probably a survival from the days so robustly described by Mr. Arliss, when, as a young actor, he braved the gallery gods of a cheap theatre on the Surrey side of the Thames; gods who devoured sausages and chipped potatoes and fried fish, the while they expressed their approval, or disapproval, of the entertainment. The popping of corks, as beer and ginger ale flowed down thirsty throats, was so continuous that it failed to disturb either the house or the stage. A hardy race of players those were, in whose vocabulary the word 'temperament' had no place. 'Acting is a bag of tricks,' writes Mr. Arliss with engaging candour; and he learned early in life to put these tricks over. His admission recalls the inspired words of George Cohan when rehearsing a doubtful farce: 'Faster! Faster! Don't give 'em [the audience] a chance to think, or they'll get on to us.'

Ellen Terry, who wrote almost as well as she played, has told us one interesting thing about audiences — that the presence of an actor in the house, an experienced man or woman who applauds with understanding, will not only quicken the intelligence of the denser crowd, but will give confidence to the players on the stage. She had herself felt this subtle influence at work, and she had heard Eleanora Duse say how sweetly and powerfully it had on one occasion affected her. The frankness of Ellen Terry's narrative, the unhesitating fashion in which she has recorded her failures, which were few, as well as her successes, which were many, is on a par with her generous and discriminating estimate of others. She knew that Booth made a masterly Iago, but that neither he nor Irving could play Othello. She considered that Irving's presentation of *Twelfth Night*, that triumph of artistic staging, was on the whole a bad production, 'dull, heavy and lumpy.' She said of her first American audiences, not that they liked the performance, but that they wanted to like it — a subtle and penetrating distinction.

The reaction of an ordinary audience reveals as a rule only the simplest emotions. It is calculated to suggest a houseful of morons, easily moved to tears or laughter, hysterical when it is not apathetic, absurd when it is not indifferent. So it was, I fancy, in Shakespeare's day (there is more than one indication of how he felt about it), and so it has been ever since. Madame d'Arblay records her annoyance at the behaviour of two young ladies who sat near her during a perform-

ance of Home's *Douglas*, and who were so much
affected by the hero's tragic death that they
'burst into a loud fit of roaring like little children,
and sobbed on afterwards through half the farce.'
One of Madame d'Arblay's companions, Miss
Weston, complained that they disturbed her more
composed distress; but Captain Bouchier was
highly amused. 'He went to give them comfort, as
if they had been babies, telling them it was all
over, and that they need not cry any more.'

Just as uncontrollable as these innocent young
things' tears were the terrified shrieks of mature
women who sat in the darkness while that 'bag of
tricks,' *Dracula*, was being shaken out — bats
instead of rabbits — straight from the con-
jurer's hat. They had come prepared to react,
and they reacted. Every absurdity of that wantonly absurd play was greeted with gasps and
shudders and hysterical laughter, as artificial
as was Dracula's mask. This sort of excitability
is conspicuous in any audience which anticipates
excitement. People who have been promised that
they will sup on horrors at the Grand Guignol
sit tense with apprehension, responding to every
ingenious device, and trying hard to get their
money's worth of panic.

A lively writer in the *American Mercury* complained a few years ago that life had gone out
of the audience, which used to be part of the show,

but which had been reduced to a state of dumb passivity. It was to remedy this inertia that Mr. Christopher Morley opened his theatre in Hoboken, and invited all who came to it to take part in the fun. His experiment was eminently successful. In five months one hundred and fifty thousand people packed themselves into the old Rialto, to see a revival of *After Dark*. They took such an active part in the fun that Mr. Morley was a little more than satisfied. 'There was real creative unity between the actors and the house,' he says. 'It was as though the footlights had vanished.'

This was exhilarating; but with the vanishing footlights there departed also that soothing silence which enabled the less strenuous portion of the audience to hear what was being said upon the stage. Mr. William Faversham was of the opinion that not since Elizabethan times had any houses exhibited such participative instincts; but he did not say that he personally coveted so lively a coöperation. Mr. St. John Ervine confessed himself delighted with the Hoboken experiment; but doubted if it would suit his cynical and melancholy plays. Mr. Morley himself admitted that the spirit of participation was apt to get beyond control. He pleaded humorously with his houses for decency of behaviour, asked that no missiles should be thrown, and protested his reluctance to call in the quieting police. Finally, Miss Jane Cowl, an outspoken actress, said plainly and distinctly that the Rialto audiences were an ill-mannered lot; that their 'fun' spelt annoyance to their neighbours, and embarrassment to the players, and that the example which they set had a bad effect upon New York theatres. It was her opinion that a 'silently receptive' house was the only one which made good acting possible.

If we turn back a page or two in the history of the American stage, we shall see no great cause to regret the polite apathy of the modern audience. It may not be 'silently receptive,' but it is — except under certain circumstances — silent. The *Mirror of Taste and Dramatic Censor*, a severe and short-lived Philadelphia monthly which was published a hundred and twenty years ago, gives us to understand that the theatre-goers of that day were for the most part a race of ruffians. Men brawled and rioted if they were drunk, and threw apple cores and nutshells at their neighbours. Women of loose character talked loudly and lewdly to their escorts. Wise men who loved the drama well enough to seek it under these discouraging circumstances left their virtuous wives at home, and wore their hats throughout the performance to save their heads from the missiles which were lightly flung about the house. There was plenty of fun to be had for the taking; but it was at the expense of the players and of the play. Not until the advent of Edwin Forrest and Junius Brutus Booth — robust men, both of them, who tolerated no disturbance — were order and quiet permanently restored.

Perhaps England was not far behind the United States in permitting, and even encouraging, the audience to be 'part of the show.' Scott, writing in 1826, says that he went while in London to 'honest Dan Terry's theatre,' the Adelphi. 'There I saw a play called *The Pilot*, taken from an American novel of that name. It is extremely popular, the dramatist having seized on the whole story, and turned the odious and ridiculous parts, assigned by the original author to the British, against the Yankees themselves. There is a quiet effrontery in this that is of a rare and peculiar character. The Americans were so much displeased that they attempted a row, which rendered the piece doubly attractive to the seamen of Wapping, who came up and crowded the house night after night, to support the honour of the British flag.'

Noisy enough these seamen must have been. But they did not racket for the sake of racketing. Some nebulous sentiment of patriotism sustained both ranks of combatants, some dim notion that they were 'carrying on' for their country's good name and their own.

It will be observed that while players do occasionally comment upon the emotions they awaken, the friendly or unfriendly atmosphere they create, they seldom or never allude to any critical estimate formed by their audiences, or expressed by those journalists who are austerely christened dramatic critics. A veteran actor has asked, rather superciliously, if anyone has ever heard an intelligent comment upon a play made by a member of the departing audience. Intelligence is a large order; but if we are content to be amused at such moments, we may have our fill of entertainment. When the curtain fell upon John Barrymore's *Hamlet,* and I was making my way out of the theatre, wondering what principle had dictated the ruthless and arbitrary cutting of the text, a lady in front of me said to her companion: 'What I liked best was that we had the play just as Shakespeare wrote it. There wasn't a line left out.' 'Oh, but there was,' said the second lady. 'I waited all evening to hear the queen say, "Out, damned spot!" and she never said it.'

Music-hall specialists, song-and-dance men, popular 'entertainers' in *revues,* establish more intimate relations with their houses than do the players of legitimate drama, who are presumably absorbed in the characters they represent. Now and then the legitimates step out of their parts, to the confusion and dismay of the cast. Forrest once dropped his rôle to tell an indifferent audience that if it did not applaud, he could not act. Irving, enraged at the reception of *Twelfth Night* in London, made an unsolicited speech, in which he favoured his hearers with his candid opinion of their understanding. On such occasions actor and audience meet on a healthy and human footing; but the atmosphere of the play is irretrievably lost. How could Forrest have returned to the noble sententiousness of *Metamora* after a display of personal vanity? How could Irving have sunk his ill-humour in the fantastic foolishness of Malvolio?

It is probable that no man living knows more about audiences than does George Cohan, and no man living has told us less. He has been on familiar terms with them since infancy. He has approached them as actor, manager, song writer, and dramatist. He has fooled them to the top of their bent. He has won them to his mood, whatever that mood might be. He has written plays as quickly as any other man could read them. He has run five companies at once with the same facile unconcern. Talented in many directions, his supreme genius lies in giving a thing a name which carries it straight through. When he called

his first song, 'Why Did Nellie Leave Her Home?'
Fortune, sniggering, took him by the hand, and
has never let go. He picked up a play by Arthur
Goodrich entitled *How Very American!* Cohan-
ized it into *So This Is London!* and ran it for
forty weeks at the Prince of Wales Theatre.
There is not a trick in the bag that he cannot
handle at sight.

It was to be expected that Mr. Cohan's remi-
niscences should deal frankly with facts. They
are, indeed, as candid as the air. The adventurous thing called life is described with humour
and relish. A strong flavour of domesticity per-
vades the volume, father, mother, sister, and
brother appearing and reappearing throughout
the narrative. Friends and neighbours and theatrical agents play their parts. The audience only
is eliminated. It was evidently something which
bought tickets, and which had to be cozened into
the belief that it had got its money's worth, and
that was all. As for every audience having a
character of its own, hateful or lovable as the
case may be; as for the 'distinct but invisible
chuckle' which heartened Mr. Arliss, the careless
cough which depressed him, the *élan*, vital and
swift, which flowed like an electric current from
the house to make his heart beat faster — such
subtleties have no place in Mr. Cohan's amused
and amusing regard.

Neither have they in Sir Johnston Forbes-Robertson's (let us give him his full designation), for that distinguished actor, who has written an autobiography as dignified as Mr. Cohan's is graceless, never mentions his audiences save when something unseemly has occurred, or when the house is graced by royalty. He tells a great many stories, but they are about people in high life (we keep genteel society in this volume); and on the last page he makes the astonishing admission that he was never meant for an actor, and never liked to act. He went through his part every night, longing for the curtain's final descent. No wonder his house — save as a paying proposition — failed to interest him. Yet this was the man who played *Hamlet* with such profound intelligence, and whose Cæsar in Shaw's masterpiece was a thing to be remembered for a lifetime. And this was the man to whom was vouchsafed the most amusing experience which theatrical gossip has to tell. It was at a London performance of *The Profligate*, and the first act was well under way, when from the stalls a voice plaintive and inebriated cried out in uttermost despair: 'My God, I've seen this play before!'

Mr. Roland Young, a very charming actor, took sufficient cognizance of his audiences to accuse them of every conceivable misdeed. They came late, they missed the best jokes, they invariably

laughed at the wrong time. A New Year's Eve
audience was his particular detestation; and it is
interesting to note that on this point most players
have agreed with him. Perhaps theatre-goers are
prone to eat and drink too much on this merry
night, and so unfit themselves for intelligent
listening; perhaps they are demoralized by the
absurd and unauthorized price they have to
pay for their tickets; perhaps men and women
who pay this price because it *is* New Year's
Eve are necessarily lacking in mentality; for one
or for all of these reasons the holiday which en-
riches the managers yields little satisfaction to the
stage.

The worst, or at least the most distressing,
misconduct on the part of an average audience is
untimely laughter. Henry James maintained that
only English-speaking people were capable of
this *bêtise*. The French were too intelligent to
blunder grossly, the Italians too sympathetic, the
Germans too well informed. He confessed that he
never took a foreigner to a serious play in London without a feeling of shame at the tittering he
heard on every side. He instanced that grim
drama, *Rutherford and Son*, as a case in point.
A portion of the house seemed to find it funny,
and laughed throughout with cheerful miscon-
ception. On the other hand, be it remembered
that a London audience, harassed beyond en-

durance by the persistent giggling of two women during a performance of *Hedda Gabler*, hissed the offenders so furiously that they fled frightened from the theatre.

When St. John Ervine's play, *John Ferguson*, was given in Philadelphia, it was received with laughter. Now I am aware that a very able writer has denied in the pages of the *Atlantic Monthly* the existence of modern tragedy. Nevertheless, *John Ferguson* is an unrelenting study of all that life holds of tragic. Not for a moment is there a ray of hope or a release from pain. It was said that women laughed from sheer nervous tension, and this was in a measure true. But they laughed principally because one of the characters was an idiot, and they considered that all remarks made by an idiot are necessarily laughable. That his uncanny prescience deepened the horror of the situation was not apparent to their minds. Miss Helen Freeman, who took the part of Hannah Ferguson, was asked how she and the rest of the cast bore this incredible lack of understanding. She said that at first they felt they could not go on with their parts; but that they had steeled themselves to concentrate their minds upon the stage, and to forget the people in front of them. In other words, the audience which stood responsible for the success of the play, and which should have been vividly present as an incentive to the players, had become a bugbear to be ignored, and, so far as it was possible, forgotten.

If this can be the case when actors and audience speak the same tongue, and there is no material barrier between them, it must be a strange and discouraging experience for a foreigner to confront a houseful of people to whose mentality he has no clue, and of whose comprehension he has no assurance. We still hear the echo of Rachel's bewilderment when she played in New York in 1855, that being the first time that the French language had been heard on an American stage. The drama was Corneille's *Horace*, and a translation had been printed in a thin pamphlet for the use of theatre-goers, who did not then sit in profound darkness. The rustling of paper as hundreds of women turned their pages at the same moment (such men as were awake being content to understand nothing) made a sound which the veteran actor, Léon Beauvallet, compared to the sudden beating of rain against a window. Rachel, at all times nervous and irritable, was driven frantic by this monotonous and recurrent sound, and even Beauvallet confessed that he preferred the somnolent silence of the male. In fact, he had for it the Frenchman's true understanding and sympathy. In his memoirs we find the first authentic notice of that great

American institution, the tired business man. 'Men who have worked hard all day,' he observed, 'do not seem entertained by French Alexandrines. If they shut themselves up in a theatre, they want gay, light plays which divert them, and distract their minds. I am far from reproaching them for their choice.'

If the foreign actor has a difficult part to sustain, the American who goes to hear a French or Italian play has troubles of his own. His one chance of enjoyment is to sit in the centre of a large and empty box, far from the madding crowd of women who are freely translating to one another in the stalls. Invariably the cultivated person who understands, or who thinks she understands, French is accompanied by one who knows she doesn't; and the whispered explanations make a sibilant undertone more distracting, if such a thing were possible, than the rustle of paper. This appears to have been a pleasant old custom, for Mr. Pepys tells us that he went to see a tragedy called *The Cardinal*, and, with his customary adroitness, managed to slip into a private box next to the king's. It was already occupied by several French gentlemen who did not understand what was being spoken on the stage; so, at their earnest entreaty, a lady undertook to tell them what the play was about. They were lively, she was solicitous, and the translating made 'good sport' — at least for the box. How the rest of the house felt about it was a matter of indifference to Mr. Pepys. He admits that he could hear little that the players said; but as the piece was 'no great thing,' he did not mind losing it. The lady and the French gentlemen were, on the whole, more entertaining.

The theatre-goers of our day would rather hear an inferior play than hear their neighbours' conversation. On this point they and the actors are in accord, though neither can compel a civilized silence in the house. Even musicians are only partially successful, with the exception of Dr. Leopold Stokowski, who has his Philadelphia audiences under such good control that they hardly dare to breathe. They sit motionless as cataleptics, would strangle rather than cough, and regard a sneeze as impious sacrilege. When a symphony is concluded they have permission, grudgingly given, to applaud. Stokowski does not hold with this boisterous clapping of hands, nor does he consider it a fitting recognition of music; but he has conceded the point out of generous sympathy with his orchestra which likes a tribute to its worth.

The 'full and understanding auditory,' which has been the desire of the actor's heart from Shakespeare's time to our own, is a boon seldom vouchsafed. The house is often full and sometimes understanding, but only on rare and happy nights is it both. Weird enthusiasms incite the drama-loving world, and dull incomprehension misleads it. Neither of these eventualities can be foreseen. The producer who keeps his finger on the public pulse is aware that his diagnosis is fallible. He stands ready to administer a merry or a dismal, a bawdy or a 'sweet pure' little play, and he does not know which will avail. The dramatist is inured to surprises. The actor plays his part in doubt and bewilderment. On the one hand, we hear Ellen Terry wondering why it was that British matrons of high estate — among them Princess Mary of Teck — would take their daughters to hear Gounod's *Faust*, but would not take them to see Goethe's *Faust*. On the other hand, we hear John Barrymore voicing a mild amazement that Americans, who had spells of virtuous recoil, 'did not seem to mind' the obvious fact that *The Jest*, which ran so successfully, 'was like a bull-fight in a brothel.'

To such enigmas the long rows of men and women sitting on uncomfortable seats in the darkness can offer no solution.

The Public Looks at Pills

SOME years ago a society of distinguished physicians and surgeons invited a well-known journalist to speak to them on 'The Doctor from the Layman's Point of View.' It was the chance of a lifetime, but the journalist made nothing of it. He filled his allotted hour with some appropriate display of scholarship (mainly Oriental), and a great many well-turned compliments. His audience, gratified but a trifle bored, expressed their sense of appreciation, and have had none but professional lecturers ever since.

In truth the layman's point of view, as it has come down to us through the centuries, is one of mockery and derision. In the pages of satire as in Hans Holbein's woodcuts, death always accompanies the physician. The French adage, 'Never waken the sleeping Doctor,' is a little like 'Never warm the frozen viper.' The old Italian epitaph, 'I was well: I wished to be better: I took medicine and died,' turns up in divers tongues and in divers ages. English comedy, like French, rings with laughter at the expense of a profession from which so much was expected that

a broad margin was left for discontent. George
Colman's sneer —

> But when ill indeed,
> E'en dismissing the doctor don't always succeed,

is forced and mechanical alongside of Gay's
swinging lines:

> Men may escape from rope and gun,
> *Some* have outlived the doctor's pill.

Dryden, more serious and assured, wrote de-
cisively:

> God never made his work for man to mend,

which was being very much at home in Zion.

The layman, writing upon the science of medicine, has never drawn any wide distinction between a statement and a fact. He gave us in the
past, as he gives us in the present, a great deal of
interesting reading which, if false to circumstance,
is apt to be exceedingly true to life. We learn
from Robert Burton, who bravely quotes authorities, that in the days of Jerusalem's might and
pride there lay open in the temple a great book
written by King Solomon, and containing remedies for all manner of diseases. To this book the
Jews had free access, and each man found in it
the cure for his ailment. But Hezekiah caused it
to be taken away, saying that it made the people
secure, and that they forgot the need of calling

upon God for help, because of their too great confidence in Solomon's wisdom.

Burton himself was far ahead of his generation in sense and rational scepticism. His words are the words of wisdom. He makes plain the advisability of dieting, which all men hate, and the unadvisability of taking other people's remedies, a habit dear to most men's hearts. Neither does he think it well for laymen to read medical treatises, and draw their own inferences. 'No one should be too bold to practise upon himself without an approved physician's consent, nor to try conclusions if he read a receipt in a book.'

Yet intelligence and marvellous erudition failed alike to eradicate from Burton's heart a dim respect for ancient cures that had nothing but length of years to recommend them. There, for example, were the precious stones. How natural it seemed to him that their beauty and durability should have power to soothe the restless maladies of the mind. And there were other substances unknown to and unseen by him, yet whose existence and qualities he could not bring himself to deny. 'In the belly of a swallow there is a stone called chelidonius, which, if it be lapped in a fair cloth and tied to the right arm, will heal lunatics, and make madmen amiable and merry.' And there were old wives' cures in which he put no faith, but which had the warrant of usage and

of error. 'In my father's house I first observed
the amulet of a spider, lapped in silk in a nutshell,
applied for an ague by my mother.' This simple
domestic remedy, though gravely recorded, is
condemned by Burton as being ill-advised. His
mother, he admits, was not the only practitioner.
He has heard of divers cures wrought by spiders.
But, after giving the matter due consideration,
he 'can see no warrant for them.'

Our world is a changing world, and the only
durable thing in it is human nature. No longer
do we put our faith in spiders, and the stone in
the swallow's belly has not even the poetic per-
manence of the jewel in the toad's head. The
diseases of the present have little in common with
the diseases of the past save that we die of them.
'Moral as well as natural maladies disappear in
the progress of time,' wrote Jane Austen flip-
pantly to Cassandra, 'and new ones take their
place. Shyness and the sweating sickness have
given way to confidence and paralytic complaints.'

Impenetrable Latin names have also replaced
the deeply coloured and dramatic words which
told a terror-stricken people in what guise death
was knocking at their door. The 'Plague,' a
strong and simple vocable, was bad enough; but
think how the 'Black Death' must have numbed
the heart with fright. The petty losses of per-
petual warfare were trivial as compared with the

blotting out of human life (one man out of every three in fourteenth-century England) when this dreadful pestilence swept the land. The *Feu Ardent* differed principally in name. We are told that the hands and feet of the infected turned 'black as coals,' and rotted away; and we know that in 1106 there was founded in Arras *La Charité de Notre-Dame des Ardents*, the members of which devoted themselves to nursing the sick until their turn came to die. Then there was the malady called, Heaves knows why, the 'Purples.' It was an afterthought in the way of epidemics, for it ravaged the town of Celle where Matilda, Queen of Denmark and sister of George the Third, was confined. The unhappy lady caught the disease from a page and died, to the great relief of those who wished her out of the reach of sympathy or succour. Even the 'Sweating Sickness,' about which Jane Austen jested, has an appalling sound which fits the horror that it bred. The Papal Nuncio, Chiericate, writing from London in 1520, says that it was so swift and sure that men riding through the streets reeled and fell dead from their horses.

Of what avail was physic against such tides of death? The world, ignorant and impotent, clung to words it could understand and feel, to remedies of childish simplicity, to the hope and consolation of prayer. Centuries passed, bringing rich gifts of knowledge, wisdom, and understanding. We seemed immeasurably remote from the helpless throngs to whom sanitation was unknown, and who stared wild-eyed at the dying and the dead. Then in our own day a pestilence, urbanely called the Influenza, carried off (so say the latest statistics) twenty million people, outstripping all recorded epidemics because of the denser population of the civilized world, and because it travelled faster and farther than any of its predecessors. When sixty-eight thousand persons died of the Great Plague in London, Frenchmen walked the streets of Paris in comparative security. The Influenza leaped a sea as easily as it leaped a street. Britain and the Balkans, Russia and Rhode Island, were neighbours in misfortune, and each and all paid their heavy toll of death.

The changelessness of humanity, which progressive minds deny, is illustrated by man's age-old inclination toward the primrose paths of charlatanism. The same spirit which made the conservative Jews seek cures from Solomon's pages impelled Londoners, who lived through the terrible months that preceded the *Annus Mirabilis*, to buy 'anti-pestilential pills,' and 'the only true plague water,' and mysterious remedies concocted by 'ancient gentlewomen,' familiar with the disease from childhood. Ambroise Paré fought a hard and, I fancy, a losing fight against the preposterous drugs of his day, the ever-popular mummy scrapings, and unicorn horns — a sovereign antidote to poison. The public was naturally incensed that a man who had risen from the despised ranks of barber surgeons should presume to depreciate such rare and costly medicines, to which only the wealthy could aspire.

In 1747, John Wesley published a book called 'Primitive Physics,' which induced eighteenth-century Englishmen to disregard Burton's warning, and 'try conclusions' on its authority. Wesley was not a doctor. He knew no more about drugs than did any other intelligent layman. But he was a popular preacher and an eminently devout Christian. His congregations naturally felt that he would not lead them astray. Moreover the volume was convenient, accessible, and far cheaper than a physician. It went into thirty-seven editions, and was consulted throughout the length and breadth of England. It contained definitions of diseases, and prescriptions for their cure. Its readers decided for themselves what was the matter with them, and took, or did not take, the remedies, which were copied from well-known medical works, with some of Wesley's personal partialities and prejudices thrown in. He warned the public, for example, against the use of chinchona bark, as 'very dangerous,' and left them to the undisturbed enjoyment of agues for which it was the only known cure. The drugs and simples that he advocated were certainly harmless if not remedial — onions and groundsel, frankincense, yarrow, and cobwebs, all of them familiar in British households. The laity has ever been loyal to its old favourites.

There was something symbolic in the long cherished belief that gold could heal all ills. We hold, in general terms, the same opinion today, but use a different treatment. The great scholar, Roger Bacon, no more doubted that gold was a curative than the great Constable, Anne de Montmorency, doubted that unicorn's horn was a preventive. Both men cherished these remedies with care. The horn cost a great deal of money, but lasted indefinitely. It came possibly from the narwhal, and probably from our old friend, the elephant. England lost faith in it, as in many other things, during the merry reign of Charles the Second; but it is pleasant to note that, in austere New England, Governor Endicott loaned Governor Winthrop a beautiful piece of unicorn's horn to insure his own and his family's health.

The most amazing tale which the credulity of the world has ever furnished is the many-chaptered history of touching for king's evil. From the days of Edward the Confessor in England (this is a matter of tradition), from the days of Clovis in France, clear down to the days of profound scepticism and dawning revolution, men clung to the belief that scrofula was healed by the royal touch. 'There is nothing that can cure the King's Evill but a Prince,' wrote Lyly in his *Euphues*; and the world, learned or ignorant, agreed with him. It was claimed that this mysterious power lay in the hands of French and English monarchs because they had been anointed with the sacred chrism; but Charles the Second, the most successful of royal practitioners, touched at Breda, Bruges, and Brussels before the Restoration; and devout believers crossed the Channel to be touched by the old Pretender — William the Third having sourly declined this prerogative of kingship.

Popularity, piety, profligacy in no way affected the healing power. The people regarded their kings as Roman Catholics regard their priests. They were conduits through which flowed certain graces, irrespective of their own worthiness or unworthiness. Louis the Eleventh was fully as conscientious in touching as was Saint Louis, and Philippe de Comines warmly commends his fulfilment of this duty. 'If other princes do not the same, they are highly to blame, for there are always numbers of sick people to be healed.'

There were indeed! Reading the records, we

should be driven to conclude that unwholesome
diet produced scrofula on a giant scale, were it not
for the fact that every kind of growth, or swelling,
or eruption — diseases described by William
Clowes as 'repugnant to nature' — was classified
as king's evil when there was a chance for the
patient to be touched. Clowes, whose office it was
to examine the applicants for touching in the
troubled reign of Charles the First, was a firm be-
liever in, and a jealous guardian of, the monarch's
prerogative. He denounced and brought to
justice an impostor named Leverett, who claimed
to be a seventh son, which he was not, and to heal
by touch. This man, a gardener by trade, had his
followers — what impostor has not! — and the
evidence showed that he had 'enticed lords and
ladies to buy the sheets he had slept in' — as
unpleasant a remedy as the annals of healing
record.

Henry the Fourth of France, who was a strong
fighter but a weakling of a doctor complained
querulously to the Countess of Guiche that, when
ill himself, he was compelled to touch two hundred
and fifty sick on Easter Day. He should have
been ashamed of his slackness. On the Easter of
1686, Louis the Fourteenth touched sixteen hundred people with little rest or respite, bearing himself as became 'a healer and a king.' The great
monarch ranks next to the merry monarch in the

number of his patients and the presumed efficacy
of his treatment. It is estimated that at his coronation he touched two thousand sick; and from
that day until his death fifty-six years later he
frequently and patiently fulfilled this strange
function of the crown. When he lay dying, a number of afflicted children were brought to his bed-
side. He was nearing the end, and his dim eyes
could not discern the wretched littie objects about
him. But two bishops guided his feeble hands to
child after child, and repeated the brief formula,
'The King touches. May God heal!' which nobly
resembled the ever-repeated words of Paré, 'I
dressed him, and God healed.'

In England the ritual for the ceremony of
touching was established by Henry the Seventh,
who began the practice of crossing the sore with a
gold 'angel,' which was subsequently hung about
the patient's neck. This custom obtained also in
France, and we might be tempted to think that
the coin was reason enough for seeking a cure,
were it not for the fact that after Charles the
First had grown too poor to give it, there were as
many applicants as ever; and Charles the Second
touched hundreds of sick before he had a spare
piece of silver for himself, let alone gold for others.
Pepys says that in the first four years of his reign
he touched twenty-four thousand people; and it is
calculated that he touched ninety-two thousand

— some say two hundred thousand — before he died. Whatever he may have thought, he always played his part with becoming gravity. What disconcerted him — as well it might — was to find himself touching when he had not meant to — *un médecin malgré lui*. John Aubrey tells us that 'a Mr. Avise Evans had a fungus nose, and said it was revealed to him that the King's hand would cure him. So at the first coming of King Charles into Saint James's Park, he kissed the royal hand, and rubbed his nose with it. Which did disturb the King, but cured him.'

Of course it cured him! That is the certain end of the story. We read over and over again that some hundreds or some thousands of people were touched for king's evil, and 'all were cured.' Now it was but natural that learned writers in the days of Queen Elizabeth should bravely assert that she healed her sick subjects. They would have been unwise to say anything else. But when it comes down to Queen Anne, who touched little Samuel Johnson, aged two and a half, we find the same repeated assurances of success. They are like the assurances of our friends today that they have been cured by patent medicines, by bottled waters, by coloured lights, by deep-sea massage, by diets as alien as King Nebuchadnezzar's, by the satisfaction of subconscious desires, and by being confidently told that they were well. It may even

have been that some rustics felt themselves cured
by the Scotch blacksmith whom Sir Walter Scott
found practising medicine (by the pure light of
reason) in Northumberland. Horrified, he re-
monstrated with the man, asking him if he never
killed his patients, and received the memorable
reply: 'Whiles they die, and whiles no. It is the
will of Providence. Onyhow, your honour, it wad
be lang till it makes up for Flodden.'

The age of credulity is every age the world has
ever known. Men have always turned from the
ascertained, which is limited and discouraging, to
the dubious, which is unlimited and full of hope
for everybody. To dream a few dreams after four
years of world war was a pardonable weakness.
To cultivate a few pleasant pretences was almost
a necessity. When Dr. Émile Coué unbottled his
sunshine to warm us, we basked gratefully in its
rays. Autosuggestion, so long as the suggestions
were of the right kind, seemed a private path to
Paradise. 'I am not a healer. You heal your-
selves,' said this delightful practitioner, and we
made haste to believe him. Faith, hope and confidence were remedies within reach of all. But
after assimilating our little horde of persuasions,
after repeating the Coué rosary until we were
lapped in content, there would come now and
then, like a cold wind from the north, the remem-
brance of words, stern and unequivocal, which we

hoped we had forgotten: 'Things are as they
are, and the consequences of them will be what
they will be. Why should we seek to deceive
ourselves?' And, shivering, we awoke to realities.

The delusions of the past seem fond and foolish. The delusions of the present seem subtle and
sane. That the seventh son of a seventh son
should have presumed to claim strange powers of
healing, and that erysipelas (which was called the
'Rose of Ireland,' like one of Moore's melodies)
should have disappeared beneath his touch, was a
manifest absurdity. So, too, was the dipping of
smallpox patients in milk, and the wasteful swal-
lowing of gold. An old Irishwoman told me when
I was a little girl that as a child she had been cured
of mumps by being driven three times in a halter
at daybreak through running water — a remedy
which modern literary slang would call 'colour-
ful.' But when a delegation of Quakers suggested
that the College of the City of New York should
establish a course of Peace Psychology, we lent
them serious attention; and when an educational
expert urged giving dolls to children as a preventive of race suicide, we did our best to follow
her line of reasoning. Two hundred years ago
doctors bled their patients to the doors of death.
One hundred years ago twenty thousand leeches
found congenial occupation in the hospitals of

London. But three years ago a man struck by a motor in New Jersey suffered himself, and was suffered by his relatives, to bleed to death, because the tenets of what he called his religion forbade his summoning medical assistance.

The perilous candour of doctors in this candid age may have lessened their prestige with the average layman, who adores pretence, and is always ready to credit what is loudly and persistently asserted. The iconoclastic jest of Dr. Oliver Wendell Holmes, 'I firmly believe that if the whole *materia medica* could be sunk to the bottom of the sea, it would be all the better for mankind, and all the worse for the fishes,' has been too often quoted by men who forget that it was spoken to the assured young students of the Harvard Medical School. Dr. Collins's criticism of a practitioner, 'If automatons could have diseases, I should select him for their doctor,' has a familiar ring. It wittily expresses a doubt and dissatisfaction common since the days of the Tudors. 'Many physicians,' grumbles Bacon, 'are so regular in proceeding according to art for the disease, as they respect not sufficiently the condition of the patient.'

There was none of this professional plain speaking in the days when newspapers were unknown, and few men were so learned and so unwise as to read books. Doctors then kept their own counsel, and left the laity guessing at the nature of diseases of which all they knew was the end. When we read that king or noble died of 'a surfeit,' we may feel tolerably sure that the diagnosis was correct. A great many people die of it now, though the word does not appear on the physician's certificate. Philippe de Comines, who gathered the strangest kind of news from every available source, tells us that Mohammed the Second had 'a swelling in his legs which every spring made them the size of a man's waist (as I have heard from those who have seen them); and the swelling never broke, but dispersed of its own accord. No surgeon could tell what to make of it; but all agreed that his gluttony was the occasion, though perhaps it was a judgment from Heaven.'

Gluttony or a judgment from Heaven? There were few maladies that could not be attributed to one or other of these causes, and occasionally to both. Charles the Bold, who was bold with caution, sought to stave off the threatened surfeit by having his six physicians sit behind his chair at table (so says the Burgundian chronicler, Olivier de la Marche), 'and counsel him with their advice what viands were most profitable to him.' They were compelled to agree, and agree quickly, with one another; but there is a story that one of them, or all of them, protested to the ducal cook that his dishes were unwholesome, to which that functionary replied, 'My business is to feed my master; yours to cure him.'

One quality has never been lacking in the long, noble, humorous annals of medicine, and it is the basic quality on which depends the worth of life — courage. The *esprit de corps*, which is unpopular on the same principle that nationalism is unpopular, has served as a fortress against fear. The heroism of the doctor who gives his life in searching for, and experimenting with, microbes is like the heroism of the explorer, the aviator, the sailor, the soldier, who all go out with high hearts to meet their duty and their death. The heroism of the doctor who gives his life in tending the pestilence-stricken is something too holy for commendation. Not for him the overmastering curiosity of the scientist and investigator. Not for him the interest so keen that it obliterates panic. And not for him the supreme joy and lasting honours of discovery. Only a sombre pathway to death, and often to oblivion. Gui de Chauliac, Papal chamberlain at Avignon and the first surgeon of his day, set the seal of glory upon his own name when he stuck to his post during the ravages of the Black Death in 1348. His *Chirurgia Magna* is the treasure of antiquarians, his admonition to physicians equals, if it does not surpass, the noble oath of Hippocrates. But because he practised what he preached, because he saw half the population of Avignon swept away, and stayed to heal the other half, his memory is honoured of men, and his soul

> Beacons from the abode where the eternal are.

In the winter of 1915 six English doctors obtained permission to visit the German prison camp at Wittenberg, and tend the prisoners who were rotting with typhus fever. These unfortunates had not seen a cake of soap, or felt the decency of clean linen, for two months. They were alive with vermin, and dead to everything but the consciousness of misery. Three of the six doctors died within five weeks; but to them and to their valiant survivors hundreds of men owed a gleam of hope, a touch of compassion, and their lives. The heroisms of the World War were beyond count and beyond praise; but nowhere was grandeur nigher to our dust, and nowhere was God nearer to man, than in that prison camp.

The late Dr. Weir Mitchell once said to me that, in his opinion, neither English nor American fiction had ever produced a satisfactory portrait of a doctor. Sevier was sentimental; Lydgate a rather dull embodiment of excellence; Thorne unconvincing as a practitioner. He was by way of thinking that the layman came no nearer to understanding the physician than to understanding medicine, though he had jested at both, railed at both, and sought help from both since the beginning of civilization. It is doubtful whether Dr. Mitchell, who was eminently fastidious, would have accepted with relish the up-to-date picture of Dr. Will Kennicott of Gopher Prairie, a plain person drawn with a firm, rough touch which consistently denies him distinction. He is often obliterated from the canvas because his wife, the exacting and pretentious Carol, takes up so much room. But the unforced realism of the scene in the Morganroth farm, the amputation by night, the flickering lamp, the inflammable ether fumes, the matter-of-fact courage of a man accustomed to take chances — this is the kind of thing we like to know is within the possibilities of daily life. It makes for confidence in a world which has always produced, and still produces, ordinary men who do the work that lies at hand. Mr. Lewis has spared no profession from the shafts of his bitter ridicule. It is he who says that managing an epidemic with a board of health is like navigating a ship in a typhoon by means of a committee. But he has given us a physician in whom we believe, and whom, if we detach ourselves from sentimentalism, we can sincerely love.

The doctor of today must infinitely prefer abuse, which is harmless, and derision, which is world-worn, to the lofty patronage of the pseudo-scientist who renders profound homage to research, and eliminates the practising physician from the field of progress. 'The fruitful study of disease,' we have been told, 'began with the investigation of Pasteur,' which is partially true. But what of Lister, who 'watching on the heights, and watching there alone,' saw Pasteur like a star on the horizon? 'The scientific use of the imagination,' a great phrase and a great quality, has distinguished many a doctor who was content to heal his fellow men. We recognize it in the words of Dr. Keen, dean of American surgery, who has registered his hope that after death he may be permitted to know and rejoice in the discoveries of the future, in the forward leaps of 'this great though little world.'

Hygiene is now the exalted idol of the public. There are none so learned, and few so ignorant, as to be without a set of rules which are unfortunately communicable. A writer in *Harper's Magazine* warned us a few years ago that there was 'no such thing as a science of medicine,' and that the study of disease was a matter 'distinctly apart from the art of healing.' 'Public health,' he wrote, 'becomes less and less an affair in which physicians should meddle. It demands rather a man of the temperament and clear-headedness of the engineer who is accustomed to think mathematically, and who dwells in a region where the landslides caused by his errors descend upon his own head.'

Do they so descend, I wonder? At least inevitably? Have there been no hecatombs of victims following the fatal weakness of wall, or roof, or bridge? It is doubtless true that 'the great majority of men who enter medicine have no intention of making their *métier* the science of the study of disease.' Somebody must serve as a medium through whom the discoveries of science, the fruits of knowledge, may be conveyed beneficially to the sick man, whose eminently selfish desire is to get well. But it is a curious verdict which would forbid physicians to 'meddle' with public health. The health of the public is in their keeping. Why then should public health (a mere resetting of words) be outside their legitimate sphere?

It is disingenuous to say that only the aloof scientist is profoundly interested in his work, and that the absence of this concentrated regard on the part of the practising physician 'chills the layman's heart.' The doctor has every reason to want to heal his patient, and he does his best to achieve this end; but no sick man can hope to be as interesting to anybody else as he is to himself. He recognizes this fact, but does not at the time accept it as reasonable and right. It might modify his discontent to know that there are other critics who, being themselves in good health, censure the same doctor for thinking too much about his patients, their diseases, and their cures. He should, they consider, take a wider, nobler, ampler view of his profession. 'The world,' comments an austere writer in the *Yale Review*, 'looks to the physician for a constructive programme of living that will appeal to the imagination and the higher emotions of struggling humanity more than to statistical reminders of success in preventing disease and in prolonging life. The physician must determine what conditions are necessary to produce great men and great societies; and then direct the steps towards race improvement.'

And while he is improving the race, a large and vague order, who is to look after the mumps and measles of the ordinary individual? Poor things, but our own, and of immense importance to us at the time.

A medical society in Chicago, having plenty of time on its hands, employed a portion of this leisure in issuing a questionnaire, asking some hundreds of people (who were not in the habit of thinking) if they preferred, and why they preferred, unprofessional to professional treatment. The answers received were with one exception — the high cost of keeping alive under the doctor's care — inexpressibly futile. They showed a peevish discontent with the possible, and a colossal faith in the impossible, which are as old as humanity. Only in the event of 'continuate and in-exorable maladies,' a terrible phrase of Burton's, is this mental attitude of service. It may in-crease pain and shorten life; but it fools us with hope until we die.

As for the recurrent murmur of protest against the prohibitive cost of doctors, it is in a measure legitimatized by our actual and urgent need of their ministrations. If we complain of the high cost of radios and motors, unfeeling acquaintances are apt to ask us why we do not do without them. This is a ridiculous thing to say, inasmuch as no-body does do without them because he lacks means. He buys them anyhow. But it can be proved that it is humanly possible for us to ride in subways, and to sleep at night without the pleasure of keeping our neighbours awake; where-as if we do not have doctors when we are ill, we are liable to the annoyance of dying.

After the World War was over, the *Ladies' Home Journal* published a paper with this patroniz-ing title: 'The Returning Doctor: He can now become one of the most potent assets of Ameri-can life.' Can now become! How, I wonder, did the returning doctor feel if he read that encourag-ing assurance! How did the British Tommy feel if he read the peerless tribute to his services writ-ten by a thoughtful correspondent of the *Times*, and quoted with delight by André Maurois:

'The life of a soldier is hard, and sometimes really dangerous.'

So it is that the public looks at machine guns and at pills.

The American Takes a Holiday

Americans never have enough of one another.

ABBÉ DIMNET

FIFTY years ago, when England had more money than she has now, and the United States a great deal less, Henry James observed that his countrymen possessed little aptitude for that 'active leisure' which was the Englishman's delight and joy. 'A large appetite for holidays, the ability not only to take them but to know what to do with them when taken, is the sign of a robust people. Judged by this measure, we Americans are sadly inexpert. Such holidays as we take are spent very often in Europe, where it is noticeable that our privilege is heavy on our hands.'

Mr. James habitually confined his observations to the wealthy and cultured classes, to that very small minority of a very big world who make the *dramatis personæ* of his novels. Moreover, though his own life was constructed after the pattern of a houseboat on the Thames, he had a deep and abiding admiration for crafts that sailed the open seas. He was by admission 'the votary and victim of the single impression, the imperceptible adventure'; but he knew better than most men the value of wider impressions and rougher adventures to the intrepid human soul. He never forgave Alfred de Musset for refusing an appointment as *attaché* to the French embassy at Madrid. 'There is something really exasperating,' he wrote, 'in the sight of a picturesque poet wantonly refusing to go to Spain, — the Spain of de Musset's youth. It does violence to even that minimum of intellectual eagerness which is the portion of the contemplative mind.'

When the contemplative mind is a French mind, it is content, for the most part, to contemplate France. When the contemplative mind is an English mind, it is liable to be seized at any moment by an importunate desire to contemplate Morocco or Labrador. It took the seductive promptings of George Sand to get de Musset so far as Venice; but Shelley's first and last impulse was for flight. The roving instinct which peopled England has for a thousand years sent her sons wandering over the earth. She has been well aware that they wander to some purpose. A wise law of King Athelstan's conferred in 927 the rank of thane, or gentleman, upon any merchant who had made three voyages to the continent. Ranulf Higden, a Benedictine monk of Saint Werburg's monastery in Chester, and one of the most veracious chroniclers of the fourteenth century, comments keenly upon the restless spirit of his countrymen and upon its consequences. They are, he says, curious to see foreign countries, and eager to tell what they have seen. They live for years in remote lands, and thrive in them. They spread themselves over the earth, and consider every region they inhabit as their own.

Certain it is that the first simple and rudimentary guide-book which we know anything about was written by an Englishman, William Wey, Fellow of Exeter College, Oxford, in 1460. It was designed for the use and benefit of pilgrims bound for the Holy Land, or for the shrine of Saint James at Compostella; and gave useful directions for the handling of luggage, the choosing of good donkeys, and the payment of proper fees. It also contained a list of foreign phrases, and told the traveller how to ask for what he wanted; how to say in divers tongues, 'Gyff me that,' 'Woman have ye goyd wyne?' and (words forever on the wayfarer's lips) 'Howe moche?'

There were not wanting then, as now, critics who denounced the wanderlust they did not share. In 1617, Joseph Hall, the good and cautious bishop of Exeter and Norwich, published a book entitled 'A Juste Censure of Travel,' the contents of which may be imagined; and in 1579 John Lyly solemnly warned his countrymen that they did ill to relinquish, even for a season, the physical and moral safety of home: 'Let not your minds be caryed away with vaine delights, as with travailling into farre and strange countries, wher you shal see more wickedness than learne virtue and wit.'

The American, whose land is too vast to permit a sense of imprisonment by waters as the ocean imprisons Britain,

This precious stone set in the silver sea,

is a less intrepid voyager. Our aviators dash for the Pole, our scientists explore venomous jungles, our archæologists busy themselves in Asia Minor, our moving-picture men disturb the domestic privacy of the tiger and the rhinoceros, our capitalists sail for Paris or London on gilded liners which supply everything men do not need, and the pressure of which adds to the burden of life. These classes fail to represent their country. Scientists and explorers are men apart. So also in their fashion are millionaires. They are not the spiritual descendants of the early settlers any more than the men and women who roam in congested Fords along congested highways are the spiritual descendants of the men and women who trekked in prairie schooners over the limitless western plains. One might as well compare the Atlantic City surf bather to the viking. The pioneers were not trekking for amusement, or in the spirit of vagabondage. They were making

homes, making the State, making the Republic.
They lived dangerously, and could bear to be
alone. The virility and sagacity of their successors are inherited from progenitors who combined
individual initiative and primitive social responsibility; who could get along without neighbours, but who had to make up their minds where
the rights of neighbours lay. To their courage,
plus imagination, we owe everything but culture
and a capacity for enjoyment; qualities which
perished from starvation during the struggle for
bare existence.

Our early American mentors were all on the
side of the stay-at-homes. Emerson, whose words
were received as gospel truths by men who had
nothing in common with his intellectual aloofness, said repeatedly that his own spirit was
spacious enough, and vivid enough, to give him
the rest and recreation he desired. He derived
this notion from Marcus Aurelius, who habitually
retired into himself as an agreeable change from
Rome. 'Travelling,' said Emerson, 'is a fool's
paradise.' What pleasant thing is not? 'The
soul,' said Emerson, 'is no traveller.' He was
wrong. The soul begins to travel when the child
begins to think. It travels far and fleetly while
the man is pinned down to one familiar spot. It
rushes onward into the unknown when he is made
ready for his grave.

Mr. John Erskine, commenting upon Emerson's certainty (when was he not certain?) that 'the wise man stays at home,' admits that, judged by this test, only extreme poverty keeps an American in the paths of wisdom. Yet there is something Emersonian in Mr. Erskine's method of recommending and enjoying foreign travel. He holds it to be a form of self-expression. He says that what we look for and find when we go to Europe is neither nature nor art, but ourselves, our true selves, which become strangely familiar to us under alien skies. He hails this revelation with delight, which is a serenely philosophical thing to do. There are those of us who are justified in preferring the exterior world — especially if it be a new and lovely world — to the recesses of our own consciousness; we seek change of vision more keenly than we seek change of scene:

> Out of my country and myself I go.

The impulse to travel is one of the hopeful symptoms of life. It indicates a touching confidence in age-old dreams of felicity. The Russian lady who said to the French ambassador, M. Paléologue, 'How hard it is to be happy in the place where you are!' had never parted with illusions. She was aware that she had temporarily lost touch with happiness; but she believed she might recapture it elsewhere. Petrarch was

driven to create the paradise of Vaucluse by the
sweet and tormenting thought that seclusion
might heal his soul of pain. When he found that
it did not (pain being the portion of the sensitive
soul), he returned to Parma, or perchance to
Rome, long enough to make him sigh anew for
solitude. That eminently prudent and practical
person, the younger Pliny, solved the problem by
building himself at his summer home near Ti-
fernum a tower high enough to lift him above all
sights and sounds which he had no mind to see or
to hear. From this eyrie he would suddenly descend to join in the uproar of the Saturnalia,
diverting himself with the coarse and clamorous
humours of humanity until he was again ready
for escape.

Americans can understand the Saturnalia better than the tower. They have no urge toward
excess or intemperance; but crowds are their
delight, and the noise and discomfort inseparable
from crowds are incentives to enjoyment. Grega-
riousness is a national trait. American life is
shot through with congresses, conferences, conventions, synods, old home weeks, boy scout
weeks, assemblies of every kind and description
that can serve to bring together masses of people
whose lives are cast apart. The 'secret' societies,
those mysterious organizations of respectable
citizens who have, we trust, nothing to conceal,

gather in thousands every year. Their numbers are so great that any secrets known to them all must be of the open variety. Their costumes outshine the lilies of the field, and would put Solomon in his glory to the blush. They carry their domestic shackles, in the shape of wives and daughters, along with them; and these ladies share in all their pleasures and privileges, save only the meetings (sacred to secrecy) and the parade.

The passion for parading is inextinguishable in the American heart. It is a simple, vigorous, childlike, manlike passion, and it is common to all classes except the military. The Elks parade, the Knights Templar, the Knights of Pythias, and the Knights of Columbus parade, the Mystic Shriners parade, policemen parade, prohibitionists and anti-prohibitionists parade, ecclesiastics parade very grandly, and babies are pushed in parade by ambitious mothers competing for a prize. No climate could be less suited than ours to these demonstrations, no populace could more thoroughly enjoy them, and no big cities in the world save ours would suffer traffic to be tied up for half a day, and the serious things of life to be shunted aside, while this solemn play goes on.

The lure of an international exhibition drew to Philadelphia in the early summer of 1926 a giant convention of Shriners. Their numbers were estimated at two hundred thousand. They seemed to the crowded-out Philadelphian to be at least two millions. The exhibition consisting at that time of brick walls and a sea of mud, these visitors who expected to be amused were compelled to amuse themselves. What they did was to parade. They paraded by day and by night, en masse and in detachments. Nervous citizens sat for hours in miles of waiting trolleys, and bemoaned their fate to motormen and conductors whom the company does not permit to blaspheme. Bands played with amazing gusto at the most unexpected hours, two A.M. for example, and at that sleepiest of all sleepy moments, seven o'clock in the morning. The players seemed never to go to bed. Lodgings were scandalously dear. Perhaps they had no beds to go to, and evened matters up by keeping the rest of the world awake.

The sober city orientalized itself as a compliment to the red fez of the Shriners. Gigantic columns were decorated with weird Egyptian symbols. Plaster camels wearing the fez cocked rakishly over one eye were perched on precarious ledges. Obese and smiling sphinxes sat about the streets. Silken banners coyly inscribed 'Lulu greets you!' hung from countless windows. The City Hall was illuminated after night-fall with red lights, like a stage inferno. Men and

women jostled one another in dense and slowly
moving throngs. They consumed untold gallons
of sugary drinks, and seemed none the worse
for them. They had come from the Far West and
from the basking South. They had travelled the
pitiless miles that divide state from state. They
had spent their time and strength and money
(a great deal of money), and they were getting
what they had bargained for — numbers. One
gathered that if there had been room enough in
the streets for them to walk, or quiet enough in
the hotels for them to sleep, the great event would
have been a failure. Occasionally a Shriner told
his neighbour that this was the seventh or the
seventeenth annual convention he had attended.
He knew how many members had met in Mil-
waukee one year, and how many in Atlanta the
next. It was his conception of a holiday. Its
incentive was companionship, its charm was the
familiar, its vaunt was vastness, and its basis
was discomfort.

'It is inevitable,' says Mr. Henry Dwight Sedgwick, 'that the mass of men who constitute the
world should hold a social creed, and believe in a
communal, cheek-by-jowl organization of society.'
The American believes in it so implicitly that all
other convictions fade into obscurity by its side.
There is an intellectual life. There is an artistic
life. There is the principle of beauty to be con-

sidered, and the austere delicacy of religion. The American recognizes these abstractions. He may even lay claim to one or the other of them. But the impelling motives which rule his conduct are derived from his neighbours. They summon him to 'pile the bricks and lay the girders of their Tower of Babel,' and he hears in the call the voice of humanity. They invite him to squander his leisure in vain activities, and he sees in the invitation the flickering wings of joy. The result is a world choked to suffocation by the strenuous whose conception of goodness and whose conception of pleasure are purely social, and who are so hard at work doing things together that they have no shadow of chance to be something apart.

It is folly to say that people in general are either happy or unhappy, because, for the most part, they are neither. They do not feel enough for happiness, or think enough for unhappiness. Critics and commentators differ widely in their conclusions on this point. Two discerning Americans, Mr. Langdon Mitchell and Katharine Fullerton Gerould, find their countrymen to be sad. Mrs. Gerould thinks they are sad because they lack a sense of liberty. They are not free men in a free land, and nothing else contents the human soul. Mr. Mitchell thinks they are sad because they are devitalized. It is not the weight of thought or the pressure of circumstance which

troubles them; but the absence of any stimulus
strong enough to win a brave and glad response.
On the other hand, Signor Ferrero considers
Americans to be a singularly happy people.
He admits that their happiness has in it no imaginative quality; but he sees in their love for crowds,
in their passion for jazz, in their fondness for display, in their cheerfulness, politeness, and good
temper, signs of exceptional vitality. They are,
he says, 'brimful of delightful elation.'

I should be more ready to believe this if the
country were less brimful of manufactured gaiety,
of optimists dispensing beatitudes, and philan-
thropists counselling mirth. When people are
happy, optimists are out of a job. When people
are pleasure-loving, they need no urge to play.
A serious article in a serious magazine on 'Amusement as a Factor in Man's Spiritual Uplift,'
does not address itself to *le monde où l'on s'amuse.*
The educator who tells us that 'play is the most
important business of life' (we know it isn't), and
that 'play makes the world go around' (we know
it doesn't), assumes that we need some powerful
urge to sport. The pacifist who in 1915 an-
nounced that 'play has a decided moral advantage
over war,' was like a man mounting a bicycle in a
shipwreck.

It is the restless sentimentalism of our day
which has set us all at work making people happy

against their wills, and against their sober judgment; denying to the dull the right to vegetate, and to the tired the privilege of inaction. The titles of books and papers upon recreational activities are enough to show their patronizing and coercive character: 'Hobbies for Parents'; 'Creative Recreation for Parents'; 'Important Elements in Cultural Leisure'; and, most insulting of all, 'Happy Hours for Old Ladies'; an insufferably genial article by an insufferably kind-hearted writer, who sees herself scattering sunbeams with every page. Some years ago a prominent rector in New York asked that holidays be made compulsory. If men and women would not take them for their own sakes, they should be compelled to take them for the sake of humanity. An enthusiastic orator at a 'Recreation Congress' assured the play-leaders of San Francisco that if they would play 'long, hard and well,' they would rule, not only the State, but the country — which is the last thing the country asks at their hands. Why should California gambol her way into supremacy over her sister states?

Yet with all this good advice and all this friendly engineering, Americans still lack a discriminating appetite for holidays. In fact, a discontented college president (who probably has more appetite than days) insists that as a nation we are less prepared for leisure than any people since the be-

ginning of time. We go away a great deal, but
where and why? If we are rich enough to fancy
that we cannot bear the cold of January, the thaws
of February, or the winds of March, we escape
these salutary forces (ability to stand up against
inclement weather is the very core of successful
humanity) by dallying in Florida or the Carolinas.
The search for climate, which used to be the weakling's job, is now the millionaire's. The midwinter vacationist has become an important factor in commercial life. His mission is to spend,
and he fulfils his highest purpose as a tax-payer.

If we compare the hordes of Americans who go
pottering around the world today with their
English predecessors who got but a little way,
and that little with infinite difficulty, we know
that the balance of delight was all on the side of
the adventurous. Byron, with the incisiveness
which was his happiest characteristic, struck the
key-note when he said, 'Comfort must not be
expected by folks that go a-pleasuring.' But
nearly two hundred years before Childe Harold's
pilgrimage, that glorious wayfarer, James Howell,
declared that the daily difficulties and occasional
perils of travel intensified its felicity. 'These
frequent removes and tumblings under climes
of differing temper are not without some danger,
but the pleasure which accompanies them is far
greater; and it is impossible for any man to con-

ceive the true happiness of peregrination, but he who actually enjoys, and puts it into practice.'

Far different is the experience of a round-the-world tourist today. He not only expects comfort, but he gets it. He is taken on leash to Europe, Asia, and Africa. He is guarded, guided, spoon-fed, and schoolroom taught. The inhabited earth has been turned into a peep-show for his benefit. He sees as much of it as is good for him, and he sees it in the close companionship of his fellow tourists. He has always some one in authority to whom he can complain if he suspects the drainage; and he is spared 'the continual attention to pecuniary disbursements,' which, according to poor Shelley who was apt to run out of funds, 'detracts terribly from the pleasure of all travelling schemes.'

'Collective consciousness,' says Abbé Dimnet, 'is prejudicial to original thought'; but nobody goes on a tour around the world in the interests of individual thought, or of individual experience. The tourist may complain of other tourists; but he would be lost without them. He may find them in his way, taking up the best seats in the motors, and the best tables in the hotel dining-rooms; but he grows amazingly intimate with them during the voyage, and not infrequently marries one of them when it is over. Even the more venturesome Americans who are travelling on their own initiative in Europe, conscientious sight-seers who climb cathedral towers, hunt up monuments, and look twice as long at a double-starred as at a single-starred picture, hunger for intimacies. They say they dislike meeting their own country people, because that is what tourists of all nationalities feel bound to say; but having met them in Paris, they go off with them to Rome; happy in numbers, and in belonging to a party too cumbrous for anybody's peace of mind.

The Ford car is held to be responsible for the holiday habits of humbler Americans who used to stay at home. It has freed them from bondage to place, and from the last lingering regard for privacy. Millions of cheap motors go bumping over the country all summer long. Their occupants eat and sleep as nomads do. Many years ago, Kinglake pointed out that the dweller in a London slum enjoys a dignified seclusion by contrast with the picturesque Arab in his tent. A summer camp by the sea, prepared for the accommodation of motorists, presents a scene of indescribable promiscuity. The Arab and the tenement house lodger are lonely beings compared to the men, women, and children who huddle under bits of canvas, with none of the space and freedom of a gypsy bivouac, and with none of the gypsy's candid affiliation with nature. Local authorities of an intolerant turn of mind have been known to object to their visitors dressing and undressing in open cars, or on the off side of open cars — a feat which requires some dexterity. Therefore are tents spread on the beach, or in mosquito-infested clearings, as signs and tokens of respectability.

A fastidious American suggests that villages by the sea, or on the highway, have some æsthetic rights, and that these rights are grossly violated by motor tramps who disfigure the landscape, and leave behind them trails of dirt and disorder. Careful officials have inspected the camps, and published some discouraging reports; the water supply doubtful, the sanitation deplorable, the campers themselves indifferent to cleanliness and propriety. So great a lover of woods and waters as Thoreau admitted that the world of Nature is more beautiful than convenient; and that while beauty stirs the lonely heart, conveniences beget civilization. There is no reason to suppose that nomadic Americans who have escaped from civilization are imbued with a love of Nature. They desecrate it rudely, and with profound indifference to the enjoyment or the distress of gentler souls. Their conception of freedom is a disregard of other rights than theirs.

In the days before the World War enriched and impoverished mankind, I was deeply impressed by the little bands of German students and German clerks whom I encountered in Switzerland. They were always on foot, carrying alpenstocks and heavy knapsacks. They were noisy, dirty, graceless, and much too frugal for popularity in a country which lives on its tourists. But what genuine delight in sombre heights and smiling valleys must have impelled them to daily endurance of fatigue and discomfort! What manliness in their activity! What inspiration in their pursuit of beauty! Compared to the rich and plethoric Germans who since the war have held eating matches in the costliest hotels of Europe, these youths revealed a purposeful intelligence and a Spartan austerity. Compared to the Americans for whom the lure of the sea means 'bathing beauties,' or a babies' parade, any man who climbs a mountain for sport seems a dignified human being. Physical fitness is a mighty asset. Viscount Grey did well to counsel the students of Epsom College not to let the radio suffice for their entertainment, or the motor deprive them of the use of their legs.

Pleasure in motion is fundamental and universal. The sense of swiftness delights all living creatures that experience it. As man is a slow-moving animal, outdistanced on earth by beasts and in the water by fishes, he has devised means to overcome his natural disadvantages. When Dr. Johnson's ponderous bulk was hoisted to the top of a coach, he expressed an artless rapture at the speed with which four horses carried him over the ground. When Tom Moore rode for the first time behind a locomotive (railways being then in their tender infancy), he was enchanted by the miracle which 'hurled' him from Birmingham to Liverpool in less than five hours. Automobiles, which at the outset were leisurely, grow faster and faster every year, yet are never fast enough to satisfy the raging and purposeless hurry of their occupants. We were thrilled to learn in March, 1931, that a British racing motorist had driven his car on the Daytona Beach speedway in Florida at the rate of two hundred and forty-five miles an hour, four miles a minute; thus breaking all records, even his own, and arousing mad enthusiasm on the part of the spectators, who saw in their mind's eye the surplus population of the world visibly diminished.

The more temperate pleasures of a holiday, the amusements offered at myriads of American resorts, are not murderous. This much must be allowed them. Neither do they awaken any spark of purpose, any dormant spirit of adventure. The sensations they afford are unrelated to life. Lamb, whose monotonous days were spent at a desk in the office of the East India Company, went mountain-mad when he found himself climbing Helvellyn. 'Oh! its fine black head,' he cried in ecstasy, 'and the bleak air atop of it, with mountains all about and about, making you giddy; with Scotland not far off, nor the border countries of song and ballad.' To feel the dark and silent hills close in upon him at night excited this London clerk, this lover of Fleet Street and Covent Garden, to sleepless transport. Hazlitt shed his moroseness as a garment when he did the thing he loved best to do — tramp the English lanes (the blessed, peaceful English lanes, not yet turned into death-traps) care-free and companionless. ' Give me,' he asks, 'the clear blue sky over my head, and the green turf beneath my feet, a winding road before me, and a three hours' march to dinner.' One doubts the clear blue sky. The 'high-piled, weather-bearing clouds of England' sweep ever overhead, changeful, foreboding, and more ineffably beautiful than the soft haze of France, or the azure vault of Sicily.

The American tourist who said of his fellow tourists: 'People who do not know how to spend their time must take what satisfaction they can in spending their money,' was as wise as he was tolerant. Spending money is a real, if not an august form of entertainment. It becomes ignoble only when we are pleased with ourselves, and expect other people to be pleased with us, because we have it to spend. Statisticians — a class of men whose statements we accept for the good and sufficient reason that we do not know how to refute them — have calculated that one fifth of the millions which Americans pay out yearly for foreign travel finds its way to Canada; that illimitable and very accessible playground whose beauty we know, and whose advantages are being continually pointed out to us. We can — so we are reminded — drive there in our own cars, keep to our accustomed side of the road, buy our home newspapers, 'listen in' to home-made music and to home-made oratory, spend our national currency, and drink what was once our national beverage. We can also save money by buying furs, provided we are adroit enough to smuggle them over the border. For these reasons, and for many others, we cannot do better, if we desire the familiar (like the sexton who took his first holiday in twenty years, and spent it in watching the sexton of the next parish dig a grave), than turn our steps to the vast Dominion which holds a marvellous future in its keeping.

Travelling is, and has always been, more popular than the traveller. Saxon kings may have recognized his worth; but his neighbours abroad and his neighbours at home have seen in him little to commend. He can no longer be charged, as in Piers Plowman's day, with 'having leave to lie,' because now everybody travels, and stories too audacious are easily discredited. But the truthful things he desires to tell, and the sensible observations he desires to make, are less welcome than were Münchausen's genial fables. When Dr. Johnson said that foreign travel added little to the interest of domestic conversation, he did not mean only that he was forced to be sometimes silent when he wanted to talk; but also that the interchange of opinions on familiar topics was broken by the intrusion of unrecognized themes. Moreover, it was not every returning tourist who had tales to tell so amusing and so immaculately free from every instructive quality as had Charles Lamb. We all love to hear of misadventures; and Lamb's experience in the London Custom House compares favourably with the experience of any homecoming New Yorker today.

A censorious American critic has gone so far as to intimate that the only men who should be permitted to go abroad are those whom such a happening cannot harm, who have no companionable qualities to lose. A stoutly constructed senator, for example, is no more affected by it than is a stoutly constructed valise. There is a little wear and tear, but no other visible result. As he went, so he comes back. 'Nor should we forget, in the ennui of his return, the indubitable blessing of his absence.'

The Pleasure of Possession

T O UNDERSTAND it in its entirety we have but to turn to the good old story familiar to our school days, but now obliterated from the arid and anecdoteless pages of Roman history — the story of the mother of the Gracchi. It is very illuminating. Cornelia received a morning call from an acquaintance who wore more jewelry than the occasion warranted. Had this lady been content with owning, or even with wearing, the ornaments, nothing would have happened; but it was essential to her enjoyment that their elegance should be noticed by her hostess; and Cornelia, being but human, retaliated in kind. She summoned her young sons, just home from school, and said vaingloriously to the visitor (who presumably had only little girls), 'These are my jewels.' It was an embarrassing moment for the boys, unless, being youthful Romans, they were accustomed to attitudinizing; but it proved conclusively that the pleasure of possession, whether we possess trinkets, or offspring — or possibly books, or prints, or chessmen, or postage stamps — lies in showing these things to friends who are experiencing no immediate urge to look at them.

Thus it is that people who have nothing in

particular are essential to the content of people who have a great deal, especially if that great deal is of the kind the purchase of which is called 'collecting.' There is no keener satisfaction in this world than the satisfaction of the collector. We hardly needed Mr. Edward Newton's ardent asseverations to convince us of this truth. To collect anything, no matter what, is the healthy human impulse of man and boy, and the longer and harder the search, the greater the joy of acquisition. I have sometimes thought that one reason why women are less content with life than are men is because they lack this eager and exhilarating passion. The natural impulse of a woman is to get rid of things. The natural impulse of a man is to hold on to them. Collecting rare manuscripts has been known to keep a wealthy consumptive alive for years. He was too absorbed in his pursuit to take the time to die. No such evasion of the inevitable is credited to a woman.

If I emphasize 'collections' over less subtle and arrogant possessions, it is because they call more imperiously for notice. A man cannot in decency point out to friends his plumbing, or his wife's pearls. He cannot tell them what these things cost, though many of us would be glad to know. But he can point out his books, and prints, and also — by an extension of grace — his wife's garden. He can, moreover, be fairly coercive in exacting attention. He can tell the history of his books, the price of his prints, and the botanical names of his wife's flowers; and he is not held to have sinned socially in making these revelations. It is true that the Honourable Augustine Birrell says that collecting is 'a secret sin'; and while a most agreeable episode in the history of human folly, its charm lies in its secrecy. Precious things must be guarded from the profane eye. 'The great pushing public must be kept out.' And he commends the attitude of his father-in-law, Mr. Frederick Locker, a discriminating, though not a wealthy, collector, who 'could no more have boasted of a treasure than he could have eaten fresh meat for breakfast.'

Mr. Locker was, indeed, a man of definite withdrawals and reticences. His intercourse was at all times as fastidious as his appetite. Yet no one ever felt the urge to show his possessions more vehemently than he did. He wanted to show them to the right people; but shown they must be. When he collected *bibelots*, he founded a Collector's Club, 'for the exhibition of our treasures at each other's houses.' When he collected books, he joined a 'Breakfasting Association,' which existed solely for the display of rare volumes and manuscripts, and which had for its patron a no less distinguished bore than the Prince Consort.

As soon as he had books enough to be called a library, he printed a catalogue — which he modestly stated to be full of errors — for the enlightenment of the despised public; and he recounted to the same public so many amusing tales about the pleasures and pains of collecting, 'a perennial joy pierced by despair,' that, as a matter of fact, we are fairly well acquainted with his collections.

There is, for example, the history of a venturesome journey undertaken in midwinter, which had for its object the pursuit of a missing leaf (the one containing Ben Jonson's verses) in Mr. Locker's Shakespeare folio of 1623. And there is the tragic tale of the Palissy dish which he bought in London for forty pounds. He had no love for this masterpiece. In his secret soul he adjudged it ugly. But Palissy was the craze, and the dish was, after some vicissitudes, transported safely to England. There it was much admired until something about the coil of the central eel awakened dark suspicions in the mind of an expert. One authority after another sat in judgment upon this eel, and finally pronounced it to be at least two hundred and fifty years younger than a Palissy eel should be. It was sold, unregretted by its owner, to an accommodating customer who wanted a 'reptile dish,' and was not otherwise particular.

Mr. Birrell, who bought books for many years, pronounced it as absurd for a man to boast of two thousand volumes as of two top-coats. Boasting is not his habit (the nearest he has come to it is the somewhat arrogant assertion that he has never entered the reading-room of the British Museum); yet we do know something about his books; a first edition of 'Endymion,' for example, and first editions of the Brontë novels, and we know nothing about his top-coats.

> Small is the worth
> Of beauty from the light retired;

and small indeed the value of collections that can be neither displayed nor described. The astute collector anticipates doing both. He displays his possessions to those who enter his doors, and he describes them for the benefit of those who stand outside.

When we come to simpler things, we find that simpler methods prevail. In the matter of gardens there is, indeed, a faint but ever-present suspicion of hypocrisy. Gardens are the domain of women, and women lack the robust assertiveness of men. They can, moreover, afford a little polite depreciation of their wares, being sure of awakening enthusiasm. Ignorant people who do not know exactly what to say when confronted by a badly printed, badly bound copy of an unreadable book, which by reason of its rarity has become more precious than rubies, wax fervid over the familiar appeal of a flower bed. They feel safe.

It will be remembered that the disingenuous author of that most charming book, 'The Solitary Summer,' would have had us believe that her garden, and her garden alone, sufficed for her content. She had no need and no desire to share it with anyone. Loneliness but enhanced its loveliness, and five months would be all too short for her intimate and secret delight.

And how did this artful lady occupy those five months? By watching and tending and gathering her flowers? Not a bit of it! By writing a book about them. By redescribing the garden which had in fact done duty as subject-matter for a previous volume. By praising in print the 'metallic blue delphiniums,' the 'towering white lupines,' the 'most exquisite of poppies called Shirley,' and a delicate assortment of roses. In a word, by showing to as large a public as she could reach the beauty that was to have bloomed for herself alone. Solitude was sweet to her that she might say to her world of readers: 'How sweet is solitude!'

It has been generally conceded that the miser — the true miser — enjoys his wealth without adventitious aid from neighbours. Hoarding implies secrecy. In the old days, when hoarding meant bags of gold, neighbours might be thieves. One thinks of Midas (an ass in all but ears which were to come later) as counting his treasures in dim vaults, safe from the eyes of men. In the present day publicity means tax returns; a result which good citizens seek to evade. But since the beginnings of riches, misers have had methods of their own for exciting and enjoying the envy of the poor. Hetty Green eluded taxes as skilfully as a blockade-runner eludes pursuit; but she never meant that men should not know and marvel at her wealth. She managed, without undue expenditure, to keep it as ever-present to the public of her time as Henry Ford's wealth is present to the public of today. And an own sister to Hetty Green is every woman whose hoardings, whatever their kind and degree, are destined for eventual exploitation. George Eliot, who was acquainted with most human and all feminine foibles, put the case neatly in her sympathetic description of the thrifty Mrs. Glegg: 'Other women, if they liked, might have their best thread-lace in every wash; but when Mrs. Glegg died, it would be found that she had better lace laid by in the right-hand drawer of her wardrobe in the Spotted Chamber than ever Mrs. Wooll of St. Ogg's had bought in her life.'

Pleasures are notoriously evanescent; but Mrs.

Glegg had secured a permanent variety. It was not, be it remembered, the bald pleasure of possession, of lace lying between sheets of silver paper in a wardrobe; it depended for its highest fulfilment upon the sentiments of surviving friends and neighbours who would one day know that she possessed it.

Louise Imogen Guiney expressed the impatient attitude of her sex when she said, 'My passion all my life has been non-collecting.' The only man I know of who resembled her in this regard was Tennyson, who was heard to say that he would not give a damn for an autograph letter of Adam's, though he might be curious to know in what characters it was written. Miss Guiney, however, unlike Tennyson, spent many years in close contact with rare manuscripts which she respected, and with rare books which she loved but did not want. Her only fall from grace was induced by a veritable likeness of King Charles the Second, 'a jolly little portrait on copper,' found in a curio shop of Bath. But who would not buy with his last shilling, and cherish with his last breath, a jolly portrait of King Charles the Second? Compared to it, chessmen, and harness-brasses, and snuff-boxes, and first editions seem empty of delight. By its side, a collection of three thousand millefiori paper-weights is powerless to please. Three thousand anything, except

dollars, is too many; but three thousand millefiori illustrate the curse of numbers. Their owner
cannot look at all of them, and the rest of us —
in a world made safe for democracy — refuse to
look at any.

I was once asked to see a collection of silhouettes, and found that there were seven
thousand of them. It was a marvellous collection.
Many were very beautiful, many were very
valuable, some had historical significance. But
there *were* seven thousand. Now seven good
silhouettes hung on a wall properly toned for
their reception are a gracious sight; seventeen are
not too many for enjoyment; but seven thousand
under one roof challenged endurance. Their
owner was courteous, kind, patient, and hos-
pitable; but he did cut off our retreat when from
time to time we made a break for liberty. Years of
his life, and apparently all of his income, had been
spent in searching for these shadow pictures in
every corner of Europe and America. The
search, begun as a pastime, had become the ab-
sorbing principle of his life. It had doubtless
given him hours of anxiety and hours of ecstasy.
Yet here was the magnificent result, the vastest
collection of silhouettes in the world; and three
visitors, dazed and fagged, trying to escape from
its vastness. My word! Cornelia's Roman friend
who was asked to look at two schoolboys had an
easy time of it.

The hostile attitude of the public toward collections is but thinly veiled by polite hypocrisies and evasions. Mr. Guedalla, who has at all times the courage of his convictions, boldly asserts that this attitude is due to the intrinsic stupidity of the things collected. They represent the unusual rather than the desirable. He finds something 'faintly perverted' in the mind of the collector for whom 'the fatal lure of rarity obscures the facile charm of perfection.' He cannot see a book bought at a high price because it has a famous misprint without being carried back in fancy to the era of the two-headed calf. He is impatient at the innocent, if unintelligent, desire of a man to own something which other men have not got; and he is more impatient, although not aware of the fact, at being himself part of the pleasure of possession. He may not want the two-headed calf; he could not have it if he did; but he is liable at any unguarded moment to have it trotted out of the stable for his inspection.

Locker was wont to say that all collectors had certain characteristics in common. They might be agreeable and well-bred men, or they might be intolerably dull; but in either case they were unmistakable. He could recognize one anywhere in a crowd. Yet if human nature is ever subdued to what it works in, surely the man who has collected seven hundred glass balls (called witch-balls in an effort to make them interesting) ought not to resemble the man who has spent a fortune on the autographs of the signers of the Declaration of Independence, only fifty-six in number. And how about the British divine known to Mr. Locker, whose collection consisted solely of halters with which notorious malefactors had been hanged? This gentleman could not possibly have had the innocent and bookish aspect of one who pursued first editions of Jane Austen. In our day, and in our lenient land, his specialty would be well-nigh unprocurable. Even states which have retained the hangman do not hang. They depend upon notorious malefactors being assassinated by other malefactors, a procedure which the *Manchester Guardian* criticizes harshly as uncivilized. Collectors of World War currency have recently complained that the field is too vast. Out of ten thousand specimens of German rag, paper, and leather money, representing every conceivable sum, only a dozen are rare enough to have any real value. Halters that have seen service in the United States are too rare to make possible even the smallest collection. Now if it were gangsters' guns!

The Unconscious Humour of the Movies

THE conscious humour of the movies is a perfectly straightforward article. There is no mistaking its intention, no difficulty in following its clue. Subtlety being an intellectual asset, film directors rightly conceive that it would be lost upon their audiences. Therefore every jest is exposed with painstaking bareness to our apprehension. Hogarth is not more explicit than is the comic reel; and if Charlie Chaplin be the only comedian capable of suggesting for a brief moment the tragic shadows that fall on Hogarth's fun, and if no living comedian can touch for even a moment his vigorous humanity, it must be admitted that the cinema is admirably adapted for carrying to their conclusions the multitudinous mishaps and misadventures which enter largely into his robust conception of humour. The pie-dish carried on the head of the flirtatious servant wench in *Noon*, and 'tottering like her virtue,' could in the film meet its inevitable fall. The pilfering rogues in *The March to Finchley* could really bore the keg, and drink the stolen beer. The stout and nervous candidate balanced so precariously in *Chairing the Member* could be overturned with a great kicking of plump, tight-gaitered legs; and the little pigs scampering with their agitated mother over the bridge could really tumble into the water. In the matter of detail, the moving picture has points of vantage over the picture which does not move.

These are the high lights of the cinema. Unlike Dr. Holmes, it need never hesitate to be as funny as it can. So highly and so widely appreciated is this fun that we have Douglas Fairbanks's word for it that on the rim of the desert Arab children may be seen trying, with shouts of laughter, to imitate Charlie Chaplin's inimitable shuffle — a tribute unsurpassed since the days of 'Lalla Rookh':

> I'm told, dear Moore, your lays are sung
> (Can it be true, you lucky man?)
> By moonlight, in the Persian tongue,
> Along the streets of Ispahan.

Mr. Fairbanks tells us also that the Right Honourable Winston Churchill told him that India (less fractious five years ago than she is today) could be won to an enduring friendship by a judicious application of films. They would exert an influence surpassing the seductions of 'Lalla Rookh' as easily as they would surpass the valour of Clive, or the diplomacy of Curzon.

This lofty purpose, this inspiring propaganda, having apparently been side-tracked, the movie disports itself on an easy level of irresponsibility. The life it portrays is not precisely the life of the stage, which has a setting of inflexible limitations (people have to be pushed together in the right place at the right time to the discrediting of circumstance), but which commands and interprets the whole range of human emotions. Neither does it in the least resemble the life we know about us, which is both complex and commonplace. The film enjoys a limitless control of accessories, and uses them with skill, artistry, and daring. The earth and the ocean are at its disposal. The aeroplanes skimming through the clouds, the secret depths of the sea, the desert sands, and the wide wild wastes of snow lend aid to the dramas it unfolds. Wherever man can go, and there is now no place where he cannot go, the camera easily accompanies him.

Perhaps it is because the marvels of the screen affect us so strongly that we are disposed to resent the unconcern of the actors. A more impossible story to film than Sir Arthur Conan Doyle's 'Lost World' could never have been imagined. Apparently it had nothing but impossibility to recommend it. It dealt with a group of daring scientists who explored a South American plateau inhabited by prehistoric monsters, which had successfully resisted the march of progress, and preserved intact their conservative habits and tra-

ditions. Now an imaginative author can write
about Dinosauria sixty feet long as easily as about
field mice and sticklebacks; but to put such
creatures through their paces on the screen, and
make them appear truly alarming, required amazing ingenuity. The producers succeeded in doing
this; and to add to the vraisemblance of the pictures they engaged the services of a small but
notable group of contemporaneous beasts and
reptiles, including the highest-salaried boa constrictor in the world, a crocodile which stood at
the head of its profession, and a very accomplished monkey.

These distinguished supernumeraries lived up
to their reputations. The boa constrictor hung
itself in graceful festoons from the huge branches
of a tree, the monkey shivered and chattered
with terror at sight of it, the crocodile swam the
shallow stream, and a superb tigress (which did
not belong to that entourage) stepped hungrily
from her lair. When the plateau was reached,
horrors multiplied themselves. Gigantic and terrible shapes crashed through the forests, engaged
one another in hideous conflict, and tore their
bleeding prey asunder. The audience gasped, but
the actors remained unmoved. *Their* business
was love-making, and they refused to allow prehistoric beasts to distract them from the matter
in hand. At each fresh peril one or other of the

suitors enfolded the girl, who had been brought along for the purpose, in a close and protective embrace. They selected moments of deadly danger for tender and prolonged endearments. The proprieties were, however, strictly preserved. When the lover was finally chosen, we were told, to our relief, that somebody in the party was duly authorized to perform the wedding ceremony, and that the young couple would set up housekeeping amid surroundings which have been best described in Bret Harte's exhilarating lines:

> Where beside thee walks the solemn Plesiosaurus,
> And around thee creeps the festive Ichthyosaurus,
> While from time to time above thee fly and circle
>   Cheerful Pterodactyls.

It remains to be observed that, although beset by fearful hazards and hardships, the lovers preserved an immaculate nattiness of costume; and that, when rescued finally from circumstances which might well have driven them to idiocy, they and their companions emerged with the refreshed and hilarious air of excursionists who have been taking a week's holiday at Margate.

A recent and very successful counterpart of the *Lost World* was *Trader Horn,* filmed in 1930. Readers of Ethelreda Lewis's book will remember its amazing inconsistencies. There were chapters that seemed as real as life itself, homely, vigorous, and appealing; and there were chapters that read as if they had been dug bodily out of Rider Haggard, and spoiled in the transmission. The most absurd episode was that of Nina, a young white woman, half priestess, half goddess, vaguely alluded to as the cruellest creature in Africa; but in reality a mild-mannered girl with a 'winning way,' who spoke English nicely, and was content to leave her exalted seclusion, and marry either of her rescuers. As a matter of fact they gambled for her, and she took the one that won.

The imperative demand for a 'love interest' in moving pictures made Nina (pronounced Niner) the central figure of the film. The lost child of a missionary, she was discovered jealously guarded and implicitly obeyed by the Isorgi, an East African tribe with magnificent warriors, a vigorous and highly resonant language, and a discourteous habit of crucifying strangers. Clad in the approved costume of musical comedy — that is to say, not clad at all — and having been exposed all her life to an African sun, Nina was bleached to a dazzling whiteness. Her fair hair fell over her shoulders. In the long days of wandering that followed her flight, in the journey through dusty desert and muddy marsh, no speck of dirt defiled even her pearly little toes. She would never need a bath while she lived.

Sixty actors, officials, and technicians took

themselves and their apparatus to Mombasa in the spring of 1929 to make the pictures for *Trader Horn*. The results achieved were marvellous. The Isorgi Falls — Horn calls them the Samba Falls — were more beautiful than anything ever seen in a film. The long stretches of the river, the jungles, the sordid villages, the terrifying savages were admirably portrayed. As for the animals and reptiles they were too numerous to be effective. Hippopotami jostled one another in the river, crocodiles clambered over one another in the overcrowded lake. Hordes of fleet-footed creatures passed perpetually across the horizon, bound apparently for a 'congress-of-all-beasts,' and fearful lest they should be late. The lovers, Nina and a young Peruvian, never had a moment's quiet courtship. Elephants, giraffes, and zebras interrupted them rudely. Lions and leopards paused on their way to the congress, and endeavoured to lunch upon the fugitives. There were evidently a great many lions in that neighbourhood, and they were delighted with their chance to be heard as well as seen. No soundless movies for them! They put their whole hearts into their roars, competing valiantly, but vainly, with the barking of the crocodiles, the trumpeting of the elephants, the beating of the savage war-drums, and the shouting of savage war-cries which drowned all other noises. A more intimidating language than

Isorgi no peaceful white man need ever want to hear.

Moving-picture experts are well aware of the popularity of animals. Every kind of beast, from a kitten which we can see at home to a goat or a goose which we never want to see at all, delights us on the screen. Its naturalness of demeanour contrasts favourably with the transparent artifices of the actor. Its mew, or its bleat, or its hiss, comes plainly from its own lungs, and does not appear unrelated to it as an actor's words appear unrelated to him. I have seen a film orator address an audience which stood behind him, so that it could face the camera while he spoke into the microphone. Now a lion knows better than to turn its back upon an antagonist and roar. It is, however, an inert animal with a single-track mind, and easily discouraged. It has a habit of standing around, contemplating the situation, instead of leaping to attack. A film director confided to the *Literary Digest*, that recipient of the confidences of the world, that actors who have to do with lions are not paid exceptionally high salaries, because they are in less peril than if they were associated with a temperamental tiger, a treacherous leopard, or an elderly and bad-tempered goat.

There are two classes of people who write about moving pictures, and both of them write a great deal, having always a keen and attentive public. The first class tells us of the marvels of mechanism and the dizzy cost of production; the second class, of the lofty ideals which animate producers, and of the educational value of films. We hear of pictures costing well over a million dollars, 'and every dollar showing'; and of cameras so immense that they cannot be worked for less than a thousand dollars a minute. These details are very satisfactory. Every true American likes to think in terms of thousands and millions. The word 'million' is probably the most pleasure-giving vocable in the language.

But when we leave business for benefactions, when we cease to contemplate vast expenses and vaster revenues, and are solemnly assured that 'the impression made by the films is greater and deeper than that of any other circulating medium,' we ask ourselves what on earth this impression is, and of what value to those who are impressed. We are even more at sea when a contributor to *Current History*, who is obviously serious and obviously sincere, assures us that the picture-hall is the 'people's university'; and that the picture itself is 'an instrument destined to take its place alongside of the written alphabet and the printed word, as among the modern world's most far-reaching social forces.'

This is saying so much that it is but fair to

conclude that some meaning underlies the words. The alphabet and the printing press gave form and substance to the secret thinking of humanity; carrying it through space and time to the book-shelf on our wall, so that the least and last of us may, if he so chooses, live under 'the distant in-fluence of exalted minds.' What have the moving pictures done to so vivify the world? Mr. Hays and Mr. Fairbanks are the only enthusiasts I know who courageously face this question, and they make the same reply. The film is to be the peacemaker of the future. Mr. Hays says that it 'will do more than any other existing agency to unite the peoples of the earth, to bring under-standing between men and women, and between nation and nation.' He does not, however, make clear the character of this understanding, nor ex-plain how the battling nations and the battling sexes are to be turned into friends by the good offices of the cinema. Mr. Fairbanks is more ex-plicit. He says that the film — the American film especially — will go further than the Geneva Conference in establishing international relations, because it represents 'the pure drama of life,' and because it shows the inhabitants of countries far remote 'how alike we all are.'

If Mr. Fairbanks means that people in moving pictures are alike, he is correct. They are. They even look alike, the women especially, because they all paint their mouths the same shape, which is not the shape that any human mouth (a self-revealing feature) was ever known to be. But if he means that living people all over the world are alike, he is in error. They are not. If ever they come to love, or even to tolerate one another, it will not be on a basis of similarity.

No Oriental, for instance, would have understood the *Thief of Bagdad*, one of Mr. Fairbanks's most marvellous and beautiful pictures. He would have recognized its setting, its fantasies, the extraordinary adroitness with which a difficult tale was told; but not the pure American sentiment which was the keynote of the telling. The ennobling and purifying influence of woman, a commonplace with us, is unfamiliar to the East. It took the wise Scheherazade a thousand and one nights to tame her ferocious lord, and save her neck from the bowstring; but one look at a beautiful princess turned the Thief, like the good American he was, into the paths of righteousness and knight-errantry.

So firmly established is this feminine tradition, this simple and amiable reverence for woman as the nursery governess of the Western world, that a sorrowing critic in Argentina has recently censured our moving pictures because they fail to support so noble and consolatory a creed; because they do not consistently present 'the splendid characteristics of American women.' It is hard to portray the 'pure drama of life,' and keep in mind an especial line of guaranteed virtues. It is hard to insure the 'sex appeal,' which is the one absolute essential in the film drama, and steer clear of all its implications. There are critics who fail to find in such dramas any splendour save expensiveness, any characteristics of which we may be reasonably proud. Mr. Philip Guedalla says that Europe has 'learned America' from moving pictures, and has unfortunately learned it wrong. Mr. Aldous Huxley analyzes the world of our 'movies' as 'a crude, immature, childish world, without subtlety, without intellectual interests, innocent of art, letters, philosophy, or science. A world where there are plenty of motors, telephones, and automatic pistols; but in which there is no trace of such a thing as a modern idea. A world where men and women have instincts, desires, and emotions, but no thoughts.'

If this criticism sounds a trifle harsh, it is justified by the language in which producers label their wares, by the fashion in which they advertise them in the press. The thrice-told tale of a wife who wants more attention than her husband is disposed to give her is described as the *Heart Cry of a Million Married Women*, which is in the nature of an overstatement. The equally familiar situation of a secretary who wants a great deal more than her employer is disposed to give *her* is unfolded in this classic line: 'She took his dictation, but she desired his kisses'; a suggestion which should keep discreet business men away from that revealing film. A picturesque Oriental tale, as respectably monogamous as the *Thief of Bagdad*, promises delusively to 'lift the seventh veil of love and hate, and reveal an ecstasy of indefinable mystery to thrill the seventh sense' — words which remind us of the transcendental ladies in 'Martin Chuzzlewit.' Even a grave story of pioneer life, as good in its way as was the *Covered Wagon*, is rendered ridiculous by the language used to characterize it: 'In Storm-Charged Splendour Surges the Day when the Sunbonnet went with the Sombrero and Six-Gun, and when Love was as Eternal as the Stars above Courageous Heads' — which also sounds like 'Martin Chuzzlewit,' and clears that immortal book from the charge of exaggeration.

These sunbursts of imbecility are not precisely new. They have been in use long enough to be discarded without any sense of loss. A few years ago a moving picture called *Grass* illustrated the finest possibilities of the camera. No better film has been given us since. It showed, with a wealth of beautiful detail, the migration of the Baktyari, a nomadic Persian tribe, in search of pasture for their herds; of the perils they braved,

of the hardships they endured, of the traditional
customs they followed. Nothing more serious
could have been conceived. Nothing bolder or
more primitive could have been recorded.

Yet this simple and accurate narrative was
headlined as 'written by an angry God, staged by
Fear, adapted by Disaster.' The stars were recorded as 'doubting,' the sun as 'laughing in
cynical glee,' the snow as 'burning like the fires of
Hell,' the sunshine as 'freezing the blood in the
veins,' the herdsmen themselves, who did as their
fathers did before them, as 'fighting a finish battle with a Mad God, on a battlefield planned by
the hand of cruel Destiny, and commanded by the
Angel of Disaster.'

This is a deplorable way to write. It is not fair
to the innocent stars, or to the unconscious sun,
or to the snow which is like snow the world over,
or to the uncomplaining Baktyari, or to God.
And surely no one can suppose for a moment that
any of these advertisements are addressed to the
mentally competent. If the moving-picture hall
be the 'people's university,' what is the grade of
its students? If, as *Current History* blithely assures us, 'the films are peculiarly fitted to the age
in which we live,' what is the intellectual status of
our day? The contempt of the producer for
public intelligence is evidenced even in the matter
of titles. He betrays a nervous preference for

words which mean nothing, and so cannot be misunderstood. When Barrie's clever play, *The Admirable Crichton*, was first screened, the management, apprehensive lest the name should suggest to Americans 'something connected with the navy,' changed it to *Male and Female*, which had the advantage of being equally applicable to *Hamlet* or to *Abie's Irish Rose*. The English comedy *Captain Applejohn* was adroitly rechristened in New York *Captain Applejack;* but, when turned into a movie, this title was felt to be too intoxicating, and was again changed to *Strangers of the Night*. Ever and always there is the assumption that the film-going public, if not actually feeble-minded, is devoid of adult percipience; and perhaps this point of view is justified. A stranger sitting by my side in a local train told me recently that she had seen a most dreadful movie the night before. 'Coarse, brutal men torturing a baby. I am a grandmother, so you can think how unhappy it made me.'

I said I was not a grandmother, but that the subject seemed to me ill-chosen. What was the name of the play?

The lady struggled for a moment with her memory, and answered, *The Luck of Roaring Camp*.

It is the habit of moving-picture magnates to lay the blame for most of their absurdities on the shoulders of the censors who are the privileged meddlers and muddlers of the country. A big New York producer said that no Pennsylvanian had any business to find fault with the movies, because he or she had yet to see one as it emerged unspoiled from the studio. We have no doubt that the unconscious humour of the censor rivals, though it cannot surpass, the unconscious humour of the producer. Perhaps the flawless touch of the *Lost World* marriage came from the censor's hand. A valiant effort was made not long ago to film a sermon, to illustrate the preaching of a highly successful evangelist who had been telling, or rather reminding, a forgetful world that the wages of sin is death. The Pennsylvania Board of Censors, disliking or distrusting sermons out of church — and who can blame them? — cut these pictures so liberally that they told no story at all, and left a bored and mystified audience in doubt as to the lesson they were meant to convey.

Mrs. Gerould was probably right when she said that nobody fit to be a censor would ever consent to be one. Yet after all his blunders are only incidental, not fundamental like the blunders of the producer who denies the intelligence of the race. What puzzles us most are the things which have been left in the movies rather than the things which have been taken out. The censor may object to a woman making baby clothes for her expected infant. He evidently subscribes to the stork tradition. But everything which has preceded and is responsible for this event is shown with candid indulgence. The number of state boards and their contrasting views make for confusion. Tess of the D'Urbervilles was hanged in one State and reprieved in another. Anna Karenina killed herself in one State and survived in another. When *Coquette* was filmed for Mary Pickford, the word 'whisky' was deleted because Kansas would not like it; and the lover was forbidden to kiss the girl on the neck because Maryland (why Maryland?) would not like *that*. New York objected to the word 'graft' in a moving picture which dealt with grafters. Pennsylvania struck out the word 'anarchist,' and substituted the word 'fanatic,' as illustrating its own standpoint. Ohio forbade a parrot to use the word 'Hell.' The film shrinks as sensitively as the radio from any approach to profanity.

The far-flung fame of screen actors and their overwhelming popularity have cast a shadow over the legitimate stage. Douglas Fairbanks met with an ovation in England. A fair proportion of the eight hundred thousand letters which Mary Pickford received in five years, and which failed to dim her spirits, or destroy her belief in the sanity of mankind, came from foreign enthusiasts. When Jackie Coogan, aged thirteen, visited

Geneva, he was honourably received by Sir Eric Drummond, and photographed under the memorial tablet to President Wilson, while the League of Nations knocked off work to get a look at him. If there were anything in Mr. Hays's theory of moving pictures and a cemented world, the United States would have entered the League the next morning.

Charlie Chaplin's personal triumphs in Europe have surpassed those of any visiting American (he is English born) since the time of Mark Twain. Peers, potentates, and politicians, to say nothing of learned institutions, have vied with one another to honour him. The paltry attentions shown to Americans whom we call 'distinguished' are insignificant compared to the homage laid by England at the feet of this versatile pantomimist whom it has loved loyally and long. In Major Ian Hay Beith's perennially delightful war book, 'The First Hundred Thousand,' Captain Wagstaffe, returning to the front after a fortnight's leave, tells his friends in the trenches that if they suppose London is thinking about them, or talking about them, they can disabuse their minds of this notion. London is thinking about and talking about Charlie Chaplin, and no one else. 'He is It!' That was in 1915. He is 'It' still, and he is apparently more 'It' than ever.

There have always been, and there are now, de-

vout believers in the educational value of films.
In France a number of children were sent to see
the pictures which told the sorrowful and glorious
story of Verdun. An effort to study their reactions through the medium of a questionnaire (a
path which never yet led to a child's heart or intelligence) was naturally unsuccessful. In Berlin
the great von Hindenburg consented to figure in a
series of moving pictures, designed to set forth the
goodness of pre-war Germany, the valour of Germany in combat, and the supreme need of post-
war Germany to be prepared against attack.
Soviet Russia has used her films for propaganda
the world over. The sharp, appealing beauty of
her films, the skill and distinction with which her
artists have reproduced dim vistas and fragments
of architecture delight the appreciative eye; but
the stories told are childish. They address themselves to the emotions rather than to the intelligence of an audience, and they presuppose a
comfortable and acquiescent ignorance of history.
A year ago the Archbishop of Prague called on
Christendom to avert war by the help of pacifist
pictures. 'Saint Paul,' he said, 'were he alive
today, would use both the silent and the talking
films to spread the gospel.' It was an advanced
view for such a conservative city as Prague; but
if there is one thing we all know better than another, it is what Saint Paul would say and do in

Moscow, Paris, or Chicago. 'Think,' said a clergyman in Utica, 'of the number of epistles Saint Paul might have sent out if the Eliot Addressing System had been at his command.'

It is only natural that the executive secretary of the American Board of Review of Motion Pictures should assert that the film of the future will be 'the leading means of social reform.' Men connected with the great industry always talk like that. I understand that it is compulsory. Mr. Hays has never lost the splendid optimism with which he took possession of the field. He is now convinced that the day of the crime film is over, and that in its time it did much to discourage lawlessness among the young by showing the inevitability of punishment. 'Moreover, the deadly weapon of ridicule has been trained upon the gangster and his kind, ridicule that stripped from the gunman and the bandit every shred of false heroism that might influence boys. Now a younger generation has risen that promises to support clean, high-purposed entertainment.'

And this in the face of bullet-riddled Broadway, and of the yearly reports that deal with schoolboy crime!

Our sense of unreality in the motion-picture hall has been enhanced by the conversational film, by the drollery of hearing sounds emanate from the lips of a photograph. But some of the sounds carry fairly well, and we are spared the long-drawn tediousness of captions. The caption writers appear to be now employed in composing advertisements. No dramatic quality has been lost in the change because there was none to lose. News reels suffer most. A stentorian voice coming from nowhere addresses the audience as though it were an infant school, explains everything that is self-evident, and bellows feeble jokes. The pictures are, however, unspoiled, and the miracle of dissolving views is still as marvellous as were the shifting sands in *Wind*, the cracking ice in *The Gold Rush*. These are the effects which make the 'movie' a wonder and a delight. John Barrymore in his adaptation of *Dr. Jekyl and Mr. Hyde* gave us perfectly contrived transformation scenes. One man melted into another subtly and horribly. But that was all he had to give. The apparent need of over-emphasis destroyed the verisimilitude of the tale. Jekyl was not Jekyl, and Hyde was not Hyde, as Stevenson conceived this dual personality; and the dragging in of a purposeless love story, where Stevenson had so adroitly excluded all troublesome petticoats, turned a powerful allegory into a dull romance. As for the scenes which purported to reveal Jekyl's fall from grace, they managed to be both offensively coarse and ludicrously inadequate. The task of the producer is to see that his film

resembles Mrs. Inchbald's celebrated description
of her own countenance, 'voluptuous without
indelicacy.' So far he has failed in his adjust-
ment.

The American Credo

THE United States is a country of diverse theologies and one creed, of many churches and one temple, of a thousand theories and one conviction. The creed is education, the temple is the schoolhouse, the conviction is the healing power of knowledge. Rich and poor, pretentious and plain, revivalist and atheist, all share this supreme and touching confidence. Our belief in education is unbounded, our reverence for it is unfaltering, our loyalty to it is unshaken by reverses. Our passionate desire, not so much to acquire it as to bestow it, is the most animated of American traits. The ideal democracy is an educated democracy; and our naïve faith in the moral intelligibility of an established order makes clear the path of progress. Of all the money expended by the Government, the billions it pays for the instruction of youth seems to us the most profitable outlay.

Mr. William Allen White stands convicted of saying that America is 'the paradise of capital.' It appears so to the casual observer; but, after all, the wide world is the paradise of capital, and has been since the stone age, when capital was a bit bulkier than it is now, and was the reward

of muscle rather than of acuteness.   America is
really the paradise of education, which is a word
to conjure by. The capitalist may be consistently
courted; but he is also consistently disliked. It is
not in human nature to regard him otherwise than
with hostility. While he flourishes, we quote
Sidney Smith's witticism, and laugh — a trifle
hollowly. When trouble comes to him (as to
other men), we begin to think that maybe there
is something after all in Emerson's doctrine of
compensation.

Aware of this universal enmity, the capitalist
seeks to buy his way into favour by gratifying
his country's ruling passion, by smoothing and
decorating those academic paths which he honours all the more if he has never trod them.
He hurls millions at wealthy colleges, having
been given to understand that it is no longer
worth his while to proffer paltrier sums. Should
he be temperamentally unfitted for such high
flights, he seeks some humble byway where he
can do the trick on a modest scale. He buys,
refurnishes, and opens a country schoolhouse,
where a little girl who never lived was never
followed by a non-existent little lamb. This is
felt to be at once a tribute to American education
and to American letters.

A somewhat similar idea must have possessed
the minds of the enthusiasts who bought and

preserved the small frame building in which Walt Whitman once taught school. The teaching was a brief and negligible episode in Whitman's life. Without training, and without any burden of knowledge, the most that can be recalled of him as a pedagogue is that he dressed neatly and wore a black coat. But the association of a poet and a schoolhouse is sacred to all good Americans. What is really striking about Whitman's youth — the fact that at thirteen he could set up type rapidly and accurately — interests nobody. We do not approve of thirteen-year-old boys being able to do anything remunerative.

If we compare the modest and deprecatory tone in which the capitalist speaks of himself, and of the business of money-getting, with the grave appreciation shown by the educator for the cause which he represents, we realize that both these experts understand and conform to their country's prejudices. I say educator as apart from teacher. The teacher may be an untrained, ill-paid girl, valiantly striving to impart what she does not know to a handful of reluctant rustics. The educator is high up in the scale, and, while as ill-paid as ever, has the proud consciousness that he is the exponent of his country's creed, of what Barrett Wendell in a petulant moment° once called the great American superstition. The addresses made every year on schools and schooling are weighted with laudations. A solemn self-sufficiency marks their periods. They deal in abstractions; but abstractions of a sacred and elevating character. Possibly they revive our fainting spirits. Certainly they please an acquiescent public which naturally likes to feel it has the right idol on its altar.

Over twenty million children attend the public schools in the United States. Their numbers are stupendous, and so are the sums spent in educating them. We can rightly claim to have the most comprehensive school equipment in the world. Is it not the plain duty of a democracy to extend to every boy or girl as much knowledge as he or she can assimilate? To extend it, moreover, on the easiest possible terms, in the pleasantest possible manner. The American child has, we are told, a right to demand that 'at every level of his instruction he will have a teacher especially trained to meet the peculiar problems of that particular period' — which is a large order. The American youth has an equal right to demand that every state college shall furnish him the higher education on a low enough level to meet his moderate mental equipment. It is not so much a question of scholarly standards as of what the taxpayer wants for his money.

The pride and boast of our country (and it is a laudable pride and boast) is the costliness of our high schools. The rivalry is keen, and no money is begrudged to these spacious and stately edifices. Four years ago a contributor to the *Atlantic Monthly* summed up the 'great American secret' — the secret of our wealth, power, and leadership — in this telling sentence: 'The grandchildren of a Finlander who trailed reindeer over the snow are able to acquire their education in a $4,000,000 high school, in a mining town in Minnesota, equipped with electric stoves to do their cooking lessons on, and with everything else in proportion.'

This is a magnificent truth, and affords the writer, editor, and reader proud thrills of satisfaction. Moreover, there is nothing the country has to give to which the Minnesota-born Finnish boy may not aspire when he leaves the $4,000,000 high school, and faces life. He may become a party boss, he may be appointed to represent the United States in foreign lands, he may appoint himself counsellor at large to the people in general, like Senator Borah. On the other hand, there is just a possibility that, with wild blood flowing in his veins, this child of the North may look unfavourably upon his textbooks, and regard his educational palace as a prison. Through the plate-glass windows he may glimpse in fancy the frozen wastes his eyes have never seen; and the image of the reindeer may appear to him more beautiful

than the rattling, gasping flivver his rich acquaintance drives. That passionate cry of Andrew
Lang's to the gypsy vagabonds who were his
sires, and who bequeathed to him unsuitable
instincts forever pulling at his heartstrings, has
found an echo in other hearts too young and
strange to worship at the shrine of production.

It is because of our unassailable enthusiasm,
our profound reverence for education, that we
habitually demand of it the impossible. The
teacher is expected to perform a choice and varied
series of miracles. The school day should hold
two days' work without crowding and without
fatigue. The child must wander at ease, yet with
close and gratified attention, through diverse
paths of learning. The world of art, no less than
the world of scholarship, invites participation.
One educational expert proves beyond a shadow
of doubt that all children can sketch, and that
what they need and should have are courses
of 'observation and representation.' They must
be taught to look at things, and to reproduce what
they have seen, whether its outlines are as simple
as a pig's, or as complicated as a lobster's. Musicians are no less certain that a child's salvation
lies in music, which, it seems, he can not only
enjoy, but compose in tender youth, just as he
can write stories and draw pictures. Dramatists

are well aware that all children can act, and conceive that acting is the only art which can give
them the coveted power of self-expression.
Rhythmic dancing and nature study demand
attention. Play-leaders, lifting their voices high
above the din, assert that play and play alone
can develop in young Americans those qualities
of wisdom, understanding, counsel, and fortitude
which our fathers ascribed to religion.

Meanwhile there are things to be taught which
arouse no semblance of enthusiasm. The harassed
teacher must see to it that her (it is pretty sure to
be 'her') artistic, athletic, dramatic, and musical
little prodigies master the multiplication table.
The multiplication table is a practical asset, and
practical assets rank high, although we are
seriously told, and evidently expected to believe,
that the old, narrow purpose of fitting a boy to
make a success of his life is no longer a factor in
education. Today the school prepares both boy
and girl for citizenship, for the service of their
country. This preparation begins with the kin-
dergarten, and ends with the last day and hour of
college. President Lowell has gone so far as to
say that we can give the world neither scholars
nor leaders unless we arouse in the heart of youth
'a love and desire for the things it has no use for
now.' A brave word which will not perceptibly
affect the horde of American undergraduates,

taking their leadership for granted, and eager only to get on.

While one set of educational experts are urging a diversity of occupations, another set, equally importunate, are demanding that more time and attention be given to studies of their selection. I read in *Education* an amazing article on the teaching of history to high-school students. Now history, while undeniably the greatest of all studies, has had a hard time of it; partly because it 'discourages and antagonizes children' — so, at least, we are told — and partly because it has been crowded out by more highly favoured work. Dr. Arnold thought himself liberal when he deducted one hour a week from the all-pervading Greek and Latin of Rugby, and devoted it to modern history. He seemed quite unable to understand why, in that ample provision of time, the students made so little progress. American schools subordinate history to mathematics and rudimentary physics, which are to them what the classics were to England.

In no wise discouraged by this somewhat cloudy outlook, the writer of the *Education* paper demands the impossible as seriously and as determinedly as though he were drawing upon the resources of Helicon. In the first place, the pupils must be given a satisfactory motive for studying history; they must be convinced that it is worth their while to bestow on it their time and attention. This done, the teacher should quicken their acquiescence into enthusiasm by arousing in their minds an appreciation of noble lives and high achievements. He should make them sympathetic on the one hand and judicial on the other. He should avoid textbooks and reiterated questions. If he desires to find out what his class knows (which is but natural), 'he should adapt his interrogations to the especial need and character of each student, and in this fashion cultivate the pupil's powers of oral description.' Indeed, 'to make the recitation really vital, the teacher should see to it that the students do most of the talking, questioning, and criticizing.' The use of the blackboard is kindly permitted him; but only that he may cover it with 'drawings and diagrams to illustrate the routes of armies, *or the plan of a mediæval manor.*'

Artist, actor, and orator, as well as instructor, this versatile genius is expected to be 'brilliant, enthusiastic, fair-minded, sympathetic, firm, and skilful in narration.' 'His lessons should be constantly enlivened by anecdotes, illustrations, stories, and dramatic postures.' He should joke with his classes 'in clean harmless fashion.' 'He should make the ancient Greeks live again in their minds.' Above all, he should have a large stock of historic details always ready for use; and, to ensure this supply, 'he must do wide outside reading, especially in memoirs and biographies.' Why, with such capacity and equipment, and with all the educational institutions of the country competing for his services (for, if such a paragon exists, there can be but one), he should content himself with the modest post and less than modest salary of a high-school teacher (even in a four-million-dollar schoolhouse), is a point left to the reader's consideration.

What, after all, is a creed without miracles, and why exalt the educator unless he can accomplish the miraculous? The need of limit, the feasibility of performance, belong to less hallowed things. Thousands of people all over the country are now asking that children should be 'educated for peace'; not in a normal way, but intensively. Dr. Abraham Flexner, it will be remembered, said definitely that children should be educated for life, and life embraces all eventualities. A director of the department of child guidance in New Jersey asks that children should be taught to enjoy life, a matter which, when I was a child, was remote from jurisdiction. The teacher's job then was to keep our enjoyment within bounds. We needed no incentive at her hands. A supervising principal of schools, who is also a sunny optimist, believes and says that students in high

schools should be taught how to marry wisely and
well. They should have especial courses designed
to eliminate sentiment, and substitute common-
sense; courses which will enable them to do for
themselves what French parents are in the habit
of doing for their children.

Cities that pay a third of their incomes for the
support of their schools are naturally unreasonable in their demands. 'The teacher,' says Mr.
Guedalla, 'is the chief executive of the American
future.' His or her business is to fit the child to
become a satisfactory member of the community.
It is with this thought in our minds that we turn
our hopeful attention from what is called the
'formal' system of teaching to the 'progressive'
system, which promises a more open outlook, and
a keener interest in all that appertains to life.
In our exalted moments we see in the development of initiative, in the 'humanizing' of education, a new and friendly link between instructor
and instructed; we visualize the unfettered intelligence as a product of mutual trust and understanding. At the same time we are aware that
such a gain is neutralized by a corresponding
loss of mental and moral discipline. The most to
be hoped for is that the intelligent child, freed
from obstructive shackles, will in time acquire a
habit of systematic thinking, and a just standard
of taste and conduct. The least that we can ask

is that he should be defended from the assault of chance desires, and saved, as a high-school student, from slipping overnight into a boy bandit and the leader of a gang.

What is called the individual trend of education, encouraging a pupil to decide which studies he likes best, or dislikes least, is a great economy of effort. Only in so far as he is attracted by, or sees the use of a given subject, will that subject be satisfactorily mastered. The enthusiastic 'progressive' sees the modern schoolroom as the happy hunting-ground of children engaged in working out for themselves their chosen problems, while the teacher remains inconspicuously in the background, 'like a breathing book of reference, able to turn its own pages, and to give an answer to every question.' Just where such children and such teachers are to be found no one is bold enough to say. Doubtless they exist. I realize the progress that has been made in the conciliating science of pedagogy when I am told that the successful educator is the one who is able to take 'the child's point of view,' and recall Barrett Wendell's dark saying, 'no normal boy ever learned anything he could avoid.' Had my teachers taken my point of view concerning, let us say, the French irregular verbs, I should have been a better and a happier child; but I should not have acquired the polite language of France.

Because the interest of the nation is focussed on education, we hear much censure and much laudation on every side; but little that is to the purpose, or that deserves serious consideration. There are critics who object to warlike pictures ('Washington Crossing the Delaware') on schoolroom walls. There are critics who object to warlike verse ('Sheridan's Ride') in school readers. There are critics who object every year to Christmas carols, because a number of taxpayers do not hold with Christianity. There are critics who think that 'a light coat of moral disinfectant' is an insufficient substitute for religious instruction. There are critics who complain bitterly that our public schools are turning out a race of young mutineers who have no regard for the established order. There are critics who pour molten waves of wrath upon the same public schools because of their slavish subservience to the established order. 'Education,' they say, 'is the propaganda department of the state, and of the existing social system.' And there are critics who now and then speak a word of truth and wisdom, as did a writer in the *New Republic* who remarked that what we ask of our schools is education, and what we get is literacy.

One thing is sure. The literate can always become the educated if they are so minded. Franklin had two years' schooling, Lincoln less than twelve months. It is as impossible to withhold education from the receptive mind, as it is impossible to force it upon the unreasoning. Certain shreds of information can be transmitted under the most adverse circumstances; but not accurate knowledge upon any subject, and certainly not the intellectual tradition which is the glory of scholarship. Every year some malcontent rushes into print with a list of queries to which high-school students have given unexpected and very ingenious answers. They have opined that De Valera was a Mexican bandit, Lloyd George the king of England, and Henry Cabot Lodge a place where societies meet. These erroneous statements have been accredited to ignorance rather than to a general incapacity for thinking. The students, at some period of their young lives, had probably heard of the three contentious gentlemen; but they had never opened the pores of their minds to even a languid interest in their contentions, and were liable to be betrayed by the misleading sound of syllables.

A young Englishman, teaching in an American school, said that what struck him most sharply about American boys was their docility. He did not mean by this their readiness to do what they were told, but their readiness to think as they were told; in other words, to permit him to do their thinking for them. This mental attitude is not confined to youth, nor to the United States. 'There is no expedient,' said Sir Joshua Reynolds, 'to which men will not resort to avoid the necessity of thinking.' The common method of escape is to choose a newspaper and stick to it; to pin our faith in matters social, political, foreign, and domestic, upon its solemn dictum; to read the books it praises most conspicuously (the chances are it praises all), to see the plays it recommends.

If the disaffected and dissatisfied are perpetually reminding us that our schools are inadequate and our system slack, there are not wanting modernists to whom all that is old is outworn, and all that is untried is reassuring. They provide the hopeful element of which we no doubt stand in need. Very recently a professor of Teachers College, Columbia University, startled an audience of high-school teachers with the assurance that they had the wrong 'dope' on the classics. 'Literature,' he said, 'must be studied at the time and under the conditions in which it is produced. Once beyond that stage, its sole interest is to those who like antiques.' The professor's list of antiques included the 'Iliad,' which is undeniably old, and Gray's 'Elegy,' which is comparatively new. In their place he recommended the contents of the *Saturday Evening Post*, as comparing favourably in merit, and capable of being studied in the very process of production.

An equally optimistic professor of philosophy at the University of New York told the New York Advertising Club that in the matter of culture the American of today could bear comparison with the Athenian in the days of Pericles. He based this happy conviction on the sale of books in drug stores. The Athenians, it is well known, had no drug stores, few drugs (Hippocrates put scant faith in them), and not a great many books. 'In all our walks of life,' said the triumphant preceptor, 'we see the evidences of an education that was not known in the past. In the newspapers, in the magazines, and on the radio are to be found the signs and tokens of the new culture.'

Another evidence of an education which was not known in the past is the all-pervading woman teacher. She has her enemies — who has not? — but she is with us to stay. Whether, as Sir Andrew Macphail vehemently asserted, 'Men of character are essential to the formation of character in boys'; or whether, as Susan B. Anthony said (and doubtless believed), 'The God-given responsibility of women is to be the educators of the race'; the fact remains that American men won't teach school, and American women will.

Perhaps some dim survival of Miss Anthony's

creed may account for the average politician's notion that one woman is as good as another for the job. If the responsibility be God-given, she can safely assume it. In April, 1931, a state senator of Pennsylvania introduced into the Harrisburg legislature a bill prohibiting the employment of married women as teachers or principals in Philadelphia and Pittsburgh schools. No word was said in this bill concerning the greater leisure or the freer mind that a spinster might possibly give to her task. The senator simply stated that there were upwards of two thousand young women in line for positions which could not be found for them; and that under these circumstances the employment of married women was an injustice. He held that a wife who was unlucky enough to be the sole support of her family should keep her post, or be appointed to a new one; but women whose husbands had work should be ineligible.

It was a perfectly sound proposition from the standpoint of economy; but what about the children? No one will seriously say that the primary purpose of our schools is to give employment to deserving young women. They are not even maintained for the benefit of publishers who have succeeded in getting the books they publish into the curriculum. The taxpayer supports them at a great expense that the children

of the nation may be educated; and the only
thing to be considered in a teacher is his or her
capacity to teach. There must be a difference in
this regard. Teachers are not like Mr. Ford's
workmen, forever repeating an uncomplicated
action that awakens no interest and requires no
thought. Mr. Ford can give preference to a married man for the good of the country; but a state
cannot give preference to an unmarried woman
unless it be for the good of the children. The
patrimony of a liberal education is their best
inheritance. It does not necessarily mean four
years in one of the great colleges which have been
unkindly designated as charitable institutions
for the rich. It means contact with a liberating
mind.

A Vocabulary

Simo was out of practice in conversing with sovereign personalities whose very speech arose from resources of judgment and inner poise.

THE WOMAN OF ANDROS

SOME years ago I wrote to a friendly author (who also chanced to be a stylist) a protest against one of the wanton assertions in which his soul delighted: 'It isn't true, and, what is more, you knew it wasn't true when you said it.' To which the answer came back prompt and clear: 'Must I explain even to you that it is not a question of what I say, but how I say it?'

Yet that man was an American, and should have felt with the rest of his countrymen that what he said was a matter of vital import to a listening, or an inattentive, world; but that the fashion of the saying was negligible, provided he made his meaning plain. In the matter of speech we are needless utilitarians. 'A language long employed by a delicate and critical society,' says Walter Bagehot, 'is a treasure of dextrous felicities.' To ask from it nothing but intelligibility is to rob ourselves of delight as well as of distinction. It is to narrow our magnificent heritage of English speech to a bare subsistence,

the only form of voluntary poverty which has
nothing to recommend it. It is to live our intellectual life, if we have one, and the social life
we must all have, upon a rather shabby assortment of necessary words, when we are rich in
our own right, and can draw at will upon the
inexhaustible funds of our inheritance.

A professor at the University of Chicago who
recently published an 'American translation'
of the New Testament, turning it into language
'intelligible to the American ear,' surrendered in
the name of scholarship (for he is a scholar),
and in the names of his readers, all claim to this
inheritance. When he substituted a bald simplicity for a rich and masterful idiom, he signified
his assent to the impoverishment of our national
speech. There are some among us who think that
if Americans cannot read the King James Bible,
they had better learn to read it. Men and women
without the tenth part of their schooling have
succeeded in doing this. Its heroic wealth of
monosyllables, which exceed those of any other
English masterpiece, should lighten the reader's
task. To understand the precise significance of
every word is not essential. To love the sight and
the sound and the glory of them is part of a liberal education.

There is no liberal education for the under-
languaged. They lack the avenue of approach to

the best that has been known and thought in
the world, and they lack the means of accurate
self-interpretation. A heedless clumsiness of
speech denies the proprieties, and surrenders
the charm, of intercourse. Chesterton says that
Saint Francis of Assisi clung, through all the
naked simplicities of his life, to one rag of luxury
— the manners of a court. 'The great attainable
amenities' lent grace to his mistress, Poverty,
and robbed her of no spiritual significance. The
attainable amenities of manner and of speech, the
delicacy of the chosen word, the subordinated
richness of tone and accent, these gifts have
been bequeathed us by the civilizations of the
world. With a 'treasure of dextrous felicities'
always within reach, frugality is misplaced and
unbecoming.

It has been more than twenty years since Mr.
Henry James gave as the Commencement address at Bryn Mawr College a matchless paper on
'The Question of Our Speech.' He did not approach this many-sided subject from all its angles.
He did not link the limitations of the ordinary
American vocabulary with the slovenliness of the
ordinary American pronunciation, and the shrill
or nasal sound of the ordinary American voice.
He did not seem to be deeply troubled by the
fundamental unconcern which makes possible
this brutalization of language. If he regretted the

contentment of too many American parents with the 'vocal noises,' unmoderated and uncontrolled, of their offspring, he laid no emphasis upon the contentment of the same parents with the fewness and commonness of the words at their command.

But for the *vox Americana*, 'the poor dear distracted organ itself,' and for 'formed and finished utterance,' he pleaded earnestly with the Bryn Mawr students, and, through them, with the nation at large. It was to him incomprehensible that a people 'abundantly schooled and newspapered, abundantly housed, fed, clothed, salaried, and taxed,' should have, in the matter of speech, so little to show for its money. The substitution of 'limp, slack, passive tone for clear, clean, active, tidy tone,' was typical of a general limpness and slackness which nullified the best results of education. 'The note of cheapness — of the cheap and easy — is especially fatal to any effect of security of intention in the speech of a society; for it is scarce necessary to remind you that there are two very different kinds of ease: the ease that comes from the conquest of a difficulty, and the ease that comes from the vague dodging of it. In the one case you gain facility, in the other case you get mere looseness.'

The phrase 'security of intention' has the shining quality of a searchlight. It clarifies and intensifies Mr. James's argument in behalf of the coherent culture of speech. He probably never heard the American language at its worst. He was by force of circumstance aloof from the more furious assaults upon its dignity and integrity. 'Amurica' he did hear, of course. It is universal. Also 'Philadulphia.' He said that he heard 'Cubar,' 'sofar,' 'idear,' 'tullegram,' and 'twuddy'— for the deciphering of which last word he gave himself much credit. But the compound flowers of speech which bloom on every side of us were lost to him because of his limited acquaintance with the product of our public schools, and with the cultural processes of street, workshop, and office. From this rich array we can cull many blossoms which he must have been happy enough to miss. 'Whaja got?' 'Wherya goin'?' 'Waja say?' 'Hadjer lunch?' 'Don' leggo of it!' ''Sall I can say.' 'Na less'n fifty cents.' 'I yusta know 'im.' 'Wanna g'wout?' All of which blendings suggest the fatal 'Dom-scum' of the greedy chaplain in Daudet's story of the 'Three Christmas Masses.'

The overworked American *r* has intruded itself upon all observers; but some have failed to notice the whimsicalities of the letter *g*, which absents itself from its post at the end of certain words, as 'goin' and 'talkin,' only to force an entrance into the middle of others, as 'ongvelope.' An Amherst

professor has informed us that the word 'girl'
may be rendered — according to locality — as
gal, göl, gûl, göil, geöl, gyurl, gurrel, girrel, and
gûrl. All of these variants he heard on the tongues
of the native-born. The No Man's Land of the
immigrant he has not ventured to invade. That
the child of the immigrant corrupts the already
unbraced speech of the child of the native-born is
a fact so undeniable that educators have recognized the danger, and have striven to counteract
it. The youthful Pole and the youthful Serb forget their own tongues without acquiring ours. I
have listened for ten minutes to the voluble utterances of half a dozen young Jews in a Fifth
Avenue bus before it dawned on me that they
were not speaking Yiddish, but what was meant
to be, and thought to be, English. 'We have
among us, multiplied a thousandfold,' says a de-
spairing philologist, 'the man without a language.'

Fifteen years ago the first Good Speech Week
was started as a protest against this careless corruption of our tongue. Its object was to awaken
in the alert American mind some conception of
what language means, and what advantages may
accrue from its preservation. Unfortunately, the
wave of sentiment which popularized Old Home
Week, and Boy Scout Week, and Mother's Day,
and No More War Day, was necessarily lacking
when so abstract a thing as speech came under

consideration. People saw the point, but could not dilate with any emotion over it.

Moreover, incidental diversions, like wearing a white carnation or revisiting one's birthplace, are easy and pleasant, while fundamental reforms are admittedly laborious. Therefore the promoters of the movement were compelled to over-emphasize its practical utility. Pupils in the public schools were told that clear, convincing speech in a pleasant, well-modulated voice was a financial as well as a social asset. 'Invest in Good Speech! It pays daily dividends!' was a slogan which might have startled Mr. James, but which was expected to carry weight with the great American public.

And 'American' is a word of wondrous import to its hearers. The educators who were striving to persuade the youth of this country to speak with correctness a language which they were obliged to admit had been imported from England, eliminated, as far as possible, the unpopular adjective 'English.' There were rare and bold allusions to the 'English tongue'; but for the most part the appeal was made for 'pure, forceful, American speech.' School-children were asked to pledge themselves not to dishonour the 'American language' by lopping off syllables, or using base substitutes for 'yes' and 'no.' The word 'yep,' as commonly heard, sounds more

like the bark of an animal than a part of human
speech. One school had an 'ain'tless week.'
Another put up a poster, 'Remember the final
G!' Shops inserted the more familiar Good Speech
apostrophes in their advertisements. Moving-
picture producers screened them with 'Topics
of the Times.' A few intelligent clergymen
preached sermons on 'The Integrity of Language,'
and 'The Sanctity of Words.' A Detroit club
registered a heroic resolution to avoid the cheaper
forms of slang — such expressions as 'Say, lis-
sen'; 'You said something'; 'I'll say so'; and
'What do you know about that?' It was felt
that when men dispensed with these familiar
and beloved phrases, they would have to think
up other phrases to replace them; and that any
thinking about the words they used every day
could not fail to be a novel and stimulating process.

'America,' says Mr. Wells fretfully, 'has partly
lost the gift of rational speech. American thought
is more hampered than we realize by the necessity of expressing itself in a language that is
habitually depraved.' This is a harsh verdict.
It might enlighten, and perhaps amuse, our censor
to know that a new remedy for such depravity
has been proposed by an enterprising publisher
in the shape of a 'Fifteen-Minutes-of-English'
club, which is warranted to give us 'mastery

over every phase of written and spoken English';
and, as a result of this mastery, 'business and
social advancement.'

I wonder what especial sanctity attaches itself
to fifteen minutes. It is always the maximum
and the minimum of time which will enable us
to acquire languages, etiquette, personality, oratory, Dr. Eliot's five feet of culture, and now the
pure well of English undefiled. One gathers that
twelve minutes a day would be hopelessly
inadequate, and twenty minutes a wasteful and
ridiculous excess. But if we will buy five books,
pay for them in instalments, and read them for
fifteen minutes a day, our vocabulary will be so
rich and varied as to bid defiance to Mr. Wells,
and to all the carping critics of Great Britain.

Not that their criticism passes unchallenged
even now. Far from it. An American free-lance
has already predicted, 'Standard English for
pedants, American for the world!' Being still
on the safe side of prophecy, this trumpet blast,
like many another, must bide its time of fulfilment. America has a formula of over-expres-
sion, England a formula of under-expression;
but in both countries we may see and hear words
oddly applied, and strained to a new purpose.
The Englishman who was asked by a professor
in an American college what was his 'slant' on a
question under dispute, professed himself as

puzzled by the word. Yet its meaning seems tolerably clear; whereas the phrase 'a spot of lunch,' which I have seen more than once in English novels, is stupid and ungainly — slang without the illustrative quality which can make slang of value. The enthusiastic American who wrote of the 'inexorable logic' of Mary Wigman's dancing turned a good word into an evil path. Because dramatic speech is always highly selective, the analysis of any form of dramatic expression calls for a pure and persistent correctness.

Words are not our personal property to be dealt with as we please. Readers of Trollope (there are still men and women in the world so favoured) will remember that when Mrs. Proudie calls the Reverend Josiah Crawley 'a convicted thief,' and is reminded by the Bishop that there has been as yet no trial, and consequently no conviction, she merely vociferates 'a convicted thief,' in such a tone that her husband wisely determines to let the words pass. 'After all she was only using the phrase in a peculiar sense given to it by herself.' On the same principle, Mrs. Eddy accused a recalcitrant Christian Scientist of adultery; and, when called on to substantiate or withdraw the charge, explained that the lady had 'adulterated the truth.'

Correctness, 'that humble merit of prose,' is

never out of place. An American critic has called
our attention to the fact that Henry James
habitually conveys his elusive and somewhat
complicated conceptions in the simplest terms at
his command. The sentences are involved; 'his
concern is to be precise, not to be clear'; the words
are plain, unpretentious, and well-bred. 'It is
the speech of cultivated England. It is the speech
of England, cultivated or not.'

This instinctive preference for the tried and
tested, for the blazed trail of language, is held to
indicate a lack of intellectual curiosity; but Mr.
James was intellectually so curious that common
human curiosity, which is part of our normal
make-up, was frozen out of his consciousness.
It was intellectual curiosity which interested him
profoundly in British speech, carried by fate to
an alien continent, and forced at the bayonet's
point upon an incredible array of alien popula-
tions.

'Keep in sight the interesting truth that no
language, so far back as our acquaintance with
history goes, has known any such ordeal, any
such stress and strain, as was to await the English
in this new community. It came over, as the
phrase is, without fear and without guile, to find
itself transplanted to spaces it had never dreamed,
in its comparative humility, of covering, to conditions it had never dreamed, in its comparative

innocence, of meeting; to find itself grafted on a social and political order that was without precedent, and incalculably expansive.'

It was a mighty experience for a tongue which had been guarded with some tenderness at home, and which had grown in excellence with every generation of Englishmen. I know of no single line which expresses the perfection of language as it is expressed in Dr. Johnson's analysis of Dryden's prose: 'What is little is gay; what is great is splendid.' The whole duty of the educated writer, the whole enjoyment of the educated reader, are compressed into those ten words.

Mr. James is not the only critic who has pondered upon the mutual reactions of men and speech, upon the phrases which have been forged by human emotions, and upon the human emotions which have been in turn swayed by the traditional force of phrases. 'If reason may be trusted,' says Mr. Henry Sedgwick, 'nevertheless its processes must be expressed in words; and words are full of prejudices, inheritors of old partisanships, most fitful in their elusive and subtle metamorphoses.'

Language then is the 'living expression of the mind and spirit of a people.' The richness of allusion in our everyday speech escapes notice; but it is not without its influence on our sub-conscious conceptions. The careless cruelty of the phrase,

'Hanging is too good for him,' echoes the conscious cruelty of the persecutor as he lives, hating and hateful, in 'Pilgrim's Progress.' The solemn swing of 'From now to Doomsday,' is heavy with the weight of mediævalism. The great traditions of Christianity have powerfully affected the languages of the Western world, and have lent them incomparable splendour and sweetness. The Spanish tongue is so full of religious derivatives that it has been called the language of prayer. Just as the Italian who cannot read sees his Bible on the walls of church, and cloister, and campo santo, so the Spaniard who cannot read hears the echoes of his creed in the words he uses all his life, and responds instinctively to their dominion.

Strange and interesting links in the story of the human race are revealed in the study of phraseology. Strange and interesting influences — national, religious, and industrial — are at work on our speech today. Linguistic idiosyncrasies are social idiosyncrasies. I thought of this when I heard an American prelate, a man of learning and piety, allude in a sermon to 'the most important and influential of the saints and martyrs.' It sounded aggressively modern. 'Powerful' is a word well-fitted to the Church Triumphant. 'Virgo potens' is as significant and as satisfying as 'Virgo clemens.' But 'important' has a bust-

ling accent, and an 'influential' martyr suggests
a heavenly banking-house.

The magnitude of a vocabulary indicates richness and potential super-eminence, but perhaps
too much stress has been laid upon it by philo-
logists. Forty years ago Max Müller awoke a
passion of denial throughout the length and
breadth of England by asserting that there were
English farmers whose vocabularies did not exceed three hundred words. It sounded incredible,
and was probably incorrect; but it set people on
both sides of the Atlantic to counting up how
many words they knew, and how many words
their children knew, thus flooding Great Britain
and the States with loosely acquired statistics. A
persevering American mother kept a record of
every coherent sound her little son uttered, and
reported that at seventeen months (an age at
which some babies get no further than googoo) he
had command of two hundred and thirty-two
words. When he was six years old, he had used in
her hearing twenty-six hundred and eighty-eight
words, and was probably familiar with a few more
which he withheld from Mamma's attention.

Differing from this careless profusion in that it
is painfully and horribly precise, the speech of
certain savages reflects to a nicety their social
conditions. Far-travelled explorers have told us
of African tribes that have a separate word for

the killing of each and every undesired relative;
one word for the killing of an uncle and another
for the killing of an aunt; one word for the killing
of a grandfather and another for the killing of a
grandson. A rich and exact vocabulary to cor-
rectly express the recurrent incidents of life.

Educated Englishmen and Americans have
generously admired the art with which the educated Frenchman uses his incomparable tongue.
Santayana says that this precision is part of the
'profound research and perfect lucidity which has
made French scholarship one of the glories of
European culture.' Henry James compared the
vowel-cutting of a French actor and orator to the
gem-cutting of a French lapidary. Lord Morley
sorrowfully confessed that the French have more
regard for their language, whether they are writing it or speaking it, than the English have for
theirs. It is a severe and conscientious, as well as a
tender and a proud, regard. It is also part of the
intellectual discipline of the nation; for France,
ever on the alert to guard this high inheritance,
is far from the danger of complacency. She
watches sharply for any indication of slackness on
the part of her educators. It is not enough that a
young man should be accurately informed unless
he can accurately voice his information; unless he
can write a clear, concise, intelligent, and well-
ordered report. A schoolboy is expected to be

what Mr. James calls 'tidy' in his speech. An actress is required to be articulate, pleasing, and precise, to give to every word she utters its meaning and its charm.

The high-pitched, artificial, and eminently ill-bred voices of many American actresses unfit them for their profession. They can act intelligently, but they cannot speak agreeably. The stage has always been the exponent of correct vocalization, of that delicacy, finality, and finish which sets high the standard of speech. It was left for an American dramatist to complain that he was compelled to rewrite his play in order to eliminate all the words which his leading lady mispronounced.

If some Americans can speak superlatively well, why cannot more Americans speak pleasingly? Nature is not altogether to blame for our deficiencies. The fault is at least partly our own. The good American voice is very good indeed. Subtle and sweet inheritances linger in its shaded vowels. Propriety and a sense of distinction control its cadences. It has more animation than the English voice, and a richer emotional range. The American is less embarrassed by his emotions than is the Englishman; and when he feels strongly the truth, or the shame, or the sorrow his words convey, his voice grows vibrant and appealing. He senses his mastery over a diction, 'nobly robust and tenderly vulnerable.' The formed and finished utterances of an older civilization entrance his attentive ear.

Next to the conquest of the world by the Latin tongue through the power and sovereignty of Rome, comes the conquest of the world by the English tongue through the colonizing genius of England. A hundred and seventy million people are making shift to converse in such English as they can master. If the mastery be imperfect, the responsiveness of these multiplying multitudes to images evoked by a world-wide tongue is the most stupendous fact in modern history. Dr. Arnold Schröer has emphasized a blessed truth when he says that the cultural connection between England and the United States has never been broken, and that their common language, as represented by their common literature, gives them a common purpose and a common delight in life. In so far as this language is the expression of jurisprudence, of democracy, of mercantile adventure, it is a strong link between nations that have builded on the same foundations. In so far as it is the medium of social and intellectual pleasures, it is a mutual inheritance and an indissoluble bond. The heaped-up gold of Shakespeare and Wordsworth and Keats is part of our spending money.